The Lawrence Welk Scrapbook

The Lawrence

Welk Scrapbook

by Susan Katz

GROSSET & DUNLAP
A Filmways Company
PUBLISHERS   NEW YORK

Contents

Introduction 6
From Farm Boy to Star 9
The Early Years 14
Lawrence in Love 19
Bubbles in the Wine 23
Television 31
Canceled! 39
The Man and the Myth 41
The Plan 45
The Welk Organization 49
The Champagne Ladies 51
Those Who Left 64
Those Who Stayed 74
Meet Lawrence's Musical Family 82
Recordings by Lawrence Welk 109
Index 111

Introduction

Thirty million people couldn't be wrong! ABC might have canceled the "Lawrence Welk Show," but they could not cancel its star, or his loyal following. He thumbed his nose at the corporate executives and became a network unto himself. His fans would follow him, no matter what station he appeared on.

Lawrence Welk fought a heroic battle to keep his show on the air, and he won. His faith in God, his determination, and his concern for the people who worked with him — as well as those who watched and listened to him — gave him the courage and strength to go out and do it himself — in the grandest and most successful way possible.

What exactly is it, in a time when musical personalities rise and fall faster than you can say "rock star," that allows Lawrence Welk and his Champagne Music just to keep bubbling along? As long as people want to dance, he says, he'll make music for them. He is the most popular musical TV host in history. He is rumored to be the second wealthiest man in Hollywood (only Bob Hope out-moneys him) — and he has one of the longest-running shows on the air.

Yet Lawrence Welk's musical selections barely reflect the incredible changes that have taken place in the music world over the past two decades. His arrangements are simple, with little flair and almost no flourishes; his "musical family" is made up of the most wholesome and even-tempered performers in the industry. His own communications with his audiences seem humorless, stiff, and — even after seventy-five years — heavily accented. He can stumble over simple words and mispronounce others, but it doesn't seem to matter. It's part of the Welk style and the very thing that make him folksy, accessible — and above all, human.

He has outlasted the big bands; his name is more familiar to millions than those of many jazz greats of the past fifty years. He says he doesn't understand the music of Dave Brubeck or Stan Kenton, and he's just as certain they don't understand his. His audiences don't want to hear "progressive jazz" anyway, they want to hear Lawrence Welk.

Being on television has not changed the basic Lawrence Welk style he first developed in the thirties. Watching him is like watching a performance in a ballroom: the music is there to be danced to, and the musicians look like they're having a good time. There is a very definite sense of personal contact between Lawrence and his audience, as if he himself knows what their interests are: old-fashioned good manners, patriotism, love of God, church and family. The music he plays certainly reflects this, for it is designed to please the whole family, with songs that can be hummed, melodies that can be easily recognized, a beat that can be followed. It's pure entertainment, not "art," a successful formula Lawrence discovered years ago, and has applied, almost reverently, throughout the years.

Perhaps, though, the real key to Lawrence's success and popularity is his unshakable faith. He's stayed with what he loves doing best, even through the difficult years of one-night stands, cheap hotels, and barely enough money for food and gas. Lawrence Welk has found that looking for the good side of a bad situation means always being able to present a smiling face and a cheerful demeanor to his audiences. Lawrence Welk and his three "families" — his personal one, his "musical family," and his family of fans — are all having fun, and it is bubblingly apparent with every note.

From Farm Boy to Star

The earliest memory Lawrence Welk has of his life on the farm in Strasburg, North Dakota, is of crawling across the floor of the sod farmhouse toward his father, who was playing the accordion. Papa Welk let his young son press down on the ivory keys, and Lawrence was hooked. It was only the beginning.

It's typical of Lawrence Welk that his first vivid images are musical in nature, because the Welks, whatever the hardships of life on the farm in the first decades of the twentieth century imposed — and harsh weather, crop failures, and poverty were common problems — always had the time, and whatever little money it took, for music.

Lawrence's parents, Ludwig and Christina, were both from the German-speaking town of Strasbourg in what is now French Alsace-Lorraine — a region with a long history of religious unrest and war over which country it belonged to, France or Germany. When they were still teenagers, Ludwig and Christina fled with their parents to Odessa, in southern Russia, to escape the horrors of the religious persecution that was the outcome of the Franco-Prussian War. There the ref-

Left: You may not recognize young Lawrence, sitting on his mother's lap, but there he is in a family portrait taken in 1903.

ugees founded a new Strasburg (as they now spelled it) on the Volga River. There Christina and Ludwig fell in love and married. As her dowry, the blue-eyed, curly-haired Christina brought her gentle, understanding nature, a deep and unfailing faith in Catholicism, and a growing warmth for her new husband. Ludwig had as much to give in return: his own devout nature, his love and affection for Christina. His family accordion and a few leather-bound Catholic missals were the only material possessions Ludwig brought to the marriage.

In 1892, the newlyweds left Odessa, once again because their small Catholic sect could find no peace from persecution. They headed for yet another Strasburg, this time in America. The journey to freedom was a long and arduous one, financed by an uncle who had already settled there. They traveled by steerage to New York, then by train and horse cart over the still-unsettled wilds of America to their final destination. They brought little with them. Their most valued possession was the accordion, which had been in the family for four generations. It had belonged to a blind ancestor who made his living as a strolling player, and had double-jointed fingers and thumbs — a physical trait that Lawrence himself has proudly inherited.

When the Welks arrived in Strasburg, a little town of 400 with a 90 percent German population, North Dakota had just been admitted to the union. The territory was still untamed and open to homesteaders. Ludwig Welk claimed his land, and built his first house out of sod. It was a simple, almost spartan house, with few amenities, but Christina made it a home. Christina gave birth to their first child to be born on American soil, John, in 1893 (two children born in Odessa did not survive the cruelties of climate and poverty that the young couple endured). Then, three more children were born, Barbara, Ann Mary, and Louie. It was too small to hold the growing clan, so a bigger house was built — still of sod, but with a picket fence, lace curtains, and all the niceties of a real home. It still stands, and Lawrence goes home at least once a year to remind himself of his roots. Agatha was the fifth child for the Welks and the first to be born in the new house. Then came Lawrence, on a snowy March 11, 1903. Two more Welks, Mike and Eva, completed this family of eight children.

Although the Welks were poor by any standards, they more

than made up for what they lacked in cash with their love for each other, their belief in God, and their music.

The brothers became good and close friends, though they had distinctly different personalities. John, the oldest, loved music — he played the accordion, the pump organ, and the clarinet — which made him closer to Lawrence; he also loved the farm and the work necessary to maintain it. Louie was a mischief-maker, the least serious, most prankish of the four. He could always be counted on to do something outrageous — and funny. Lawrence and Mike were closest in age and temperament — quiet, determined, and obedient sons. Their love for each other, as well as for their sisters and their parents, was encouraged and returned by Ludwig and Christina. Papa was a true patriarch: stern and strict, but not without humor and warmth. Mama was more yielding and demonstrative. Between them, they struck a happy balance.

Religion was very important to this community of immigrants, and the center of life in Strasburg was St. Peter's and St. Paul's Church. The Welks attended Sunday mass every week, even when the harsh winter temperatures went down to thirty or forty degrees below zero. Lawrence loved the church, as much for its exceptional choir as for the inspiration and guidance he found there. The music was very special; unusually beautiful, it drew listeners from near and far. But even without the music, Sunday mass was not to be missed. The family would pile into the sleigh, wrap themselves in rugs and blankets, with hot rocks at their feet for added warmth, and arrive at the church, snug and eager. It became a pattern that Lawrence has followed all his life. He rarely misses Sunday mass, even today. All his accomplishments, and all his actions, have, in one way or another, been based on his deep and abiding faith. This is a legacy he has passed on to his own children.

Though the family may not always have had enough to eat — sometimes, supper was only bread and milk — they did have, beside their faith and each other, their music. Somehow, they had saved enough to buy a small pump organ. Lawrence learned to play the instrument when he was four years old: the time when his feet could reach the pedals. He loved to hear his father play, and remembers Papa's habit of starting the beat by tapping his foot to the count of three. Even today, Lawrence does the same — "And-a one, and a-two, and a-three" — before he brings down the baton.

The world of music was, to young Lawrence, a safe place, one where he was happy and secure — whether he was fashioning "violins" out of old boxes and horsehair, or sitting at his father's feet while the family gathered round for a musical evening of singing and playing. Every minute he was not doing his farm chores — lugging water, milking the cows, feeding the hogs (all of which he disliked) — he was doing something musical. It made up for his feeling that he was inferior to the rest of his family — that he was the smallest, skinniest, and homeliest Welk.

Lawrence was a sickly child, and was well past seven before he started at the Strasburg school, run by Ursuline nuns. Although they taught in German, they also tried to teach their charges the English language. It was a valiant effort, but often it failed. The community spoke German, for the most part, and it was the only language spoken in the Welk home. Lawrence didn't really learn to speak English well until he was twenty-one, and he still speaks with an accent — particularly when he's excited or angry. Never much of a scholar, when he was eleven years old, a ruptured appendix, followed by peritonitis, kept him out of school for a year. He then decided he had had enough education and quit school altogether. He would have had to repeat the fourth grade, with classmates a year or two younger than he, which would have been much too embarrassing. His parents agreed to let him stay home and work on the farm, thankful that he pulled through an illness that, in 1914, was often fatal.

It was while he was convalescing that he made the biggest decision in his life. Someday, as soon as he was able, he would leave the farm and take up the life of a musician. He had never had a formal music lesson; he didn't even have his own accordion to play — Papa's was too much of an heirloom for a youngster to handle, and his brother, John, didn't want to lend his to the aspiring musician. Carefully saving every penny that he could earn by trapping animals and selling the skins and meat, Lawrence finally collected the fifteen dollars he needed to send away for his first accordion — selected from a mail-order catalog. He started playing at local dances and weddings — some of which lasted as long as three days. The accordion soon started showing the wear and tear of the heavy use and actually fell apart! Again, Lawrence saved enough money to send away for another, more expensive model. This one cost twenty dollars, but it didn't last much longer than the first one. Now Lawrence was desperate. He needed an accordion that would hold up under the strain of the numerous church socials, weddings, and barn dances. His neighbors were a dancing bunch, and nothing pleased them more than rousing polka after rousing polka.

Somewhat hesitantly, Lawrence went to his father and asked him for help. Would he lend Lawrence $400 for a real accordion? A tough bargain was struck between father and son. Lawrence would work for four years on the farm without pay in order to pay off the loan and any money Lawrence made from his music would go to his father. But it was all worth it to Lawrence, who loved nothing better than the music he could squeeze from his own accordion. Music was becoming his life.

The Hotsy Totsy Boys — America's Biggest Little Band, was Lawrence's first orchestra.

The Early Years

On March 11, 1924, his twenty-first birthday, Lawrence Welk left home to find fame and fortune. He had only enough money to take him as far as Aberdeen, South Dakota — not terribly far away. Neither recognition nor dollars came instantly. Playing at dances and weddings barely paid enough to eat. So Lawrence joined the "Jazzy Junior Five," a group of eleven- and twelve-year-olds, adding his accordion to the other instruments until he made enough money to move on to Bismarck, North Dakota — a larger town with larger opportunities. After finding a job in a music store, which helped supplement the meager income he eked out by playing, he met Frank Schalk, a drummer, and the two joined forces. They soon joined up with the "Lincoln Boulds Orchestra." It was an experience that left Lawrence richer in some ways (he learned how to read music and how *not* to run an orchestra) and poorer in others (when he left the band, Boulds still owed him $600, which he never collected). It was here that Lawrence decided he would always make sure that *he* could pay *his* musicians.

Lawrence took off, in the summer of 1925, for a lake resort

in Iowa. It had seven dance pavilions, with continuous dancing, and Lawrence went on with his self-education. He watched and learned what pleases an audience, and why, out of the seven orchestras, only a couple of them drew the crowds. It was a valuable few months. Armed with this new insight into the world of dance bands, Lawrence went back to Aberdeen, determined to form one of his own. However, before he could, fate (or good luck) intervened in the person of George T. Kelly, an itinerant showman. Kelly, with his wife Alma, and another couple, made up the "Peerless Entertainers." Kelly liked Lawrence's musical style, and invited him to join his merry band of thespians, not just as an accordionist, but as an actor, too. It was a lucky invitation. Travel-

Though their professional careers were just beginning, the orchestra members found that posing for pictures came quite naturally. Also, it was quite fun!

ing with Kelly taught Lawrence more about show business than he could have ever hoped to know. He learned not only how to get along with people and how to make a lasting impression, but also how to butter up dance hall and theater owners to guarantee a well-paying crowd. He would call in advance to confirm a booking, and, at the same time, suggest some ways to advertise the appearance free — to his and the bookers' advantage.

Alma Kelly also taught him to speak English, not an inconsiderable accomplishment. Today, decades later, Lawrence Welk speaks with great admiration and fondness for his mentors and what they taught him. Among the valuable lessons, the most important was a basic truth about human nature — that a good impression is a remembered one, and if you show consideration toward your fellow man, you'll get it back in kind. It's one of the basic principles Lawrence has followed all his life, along with those special ones he learned from his industrious father: hard work, striving for quality,

The six-piece ensemble, with Lawrence on the accordion, of course, played all over the Midwest, and played on the radio as often as they could.

and always having at least one goal in mind.

The apprenticeship with the "Peerless Entertainers" ended when Kelly went off on one "bender" too many. Kelly took a kind of forced retirement, and the band dissolved. Lawrence went back to Bismarck where he finally formed his first orchestra. It was 1927, and "Lawrence Welk and His Hotsy Totsy Boys — The Biggest Little Band in America" arrived in Yankton, South Dakota, ready for success. But the money was scarce, and the bookings even more so. Lawrence was determined to have his big chance, and the radio station WNAX gave it to him. His first broadcast, which was just to have been an audition, was so well received, that the boys were not only booked for appearances in dance halls all over the listening area, but made WNAX keep them on the air for six years. The little orchestra was growing, and so was Lawrence. He learned to play a little piano, saxophone, banjo, organ, and drums, so he could fill in whenever another musician was needed.

Lawrence in Love

It was during the first year in Yankton that Lawrence met the person who was to mean the most to him throughout his life. Her name was Fern Renner, and she was a nursing student at Sacred Heart Hospital in Yankton. She hoped to become a doctor someday, or to go into medical research — getting involved with a bandleader was not in her plans.

Fern Renner not only had no room in her life for dating a traveling musician, but, as she recalls, she wasn't interested in seeing him perform. She had to be dragged to a dance by her fellow student nurses to find out about the tall, handsome local matinee idol who had won the hearts of all her girlfriends with his twice-a-day radio shows and personal appearances. Though not overly impressed, Fern did agree to have dinner with him — if he got her home early enough to study. Apparently, Fern was the only girl in Yankton who did not have romantic designs on "Lawrence with the flashing eyes."

Fern began to get a glimmer that perhaps Lawrence was more than just casually interested in her when he checked

Left: It's easy to see why the ladies loved Lawrence. He had a beautiful smile, expressive eyes, and was a handsome fellow by any standards.

himself into the hospital she worked in for an operation on his tonsils. It was a necessary, but not an emergency, procedure, and he did it really to make Fern notice him more. He managed to get a room on the floor she was usually assigned to; but as luck would have it, student nurses did not care for postoperative patients, and Fern was nowhere in sight. She did, however, admire his perseverance, and came to visit. They soon became close friends.

When Lawrence was released from the hospital, they began to date, but not seriously. Fern accepted a job in Dallas after graduation, and Lawrence had engagements booked in Lake Placid and Denver. There was definitely something happening romantically for them, but it hadn't really taken shape yet.

Lawrence wrote often while he was on the road, and this told her just how serious his intentions were becoming. She knew it was difficult enough for him to speak English, but to write it . . . that surely said the man meant to be more than just another beau. On her way home to Yankton for a vacation, Fern stopped off to visit Lawrence in Denver. He proposed. She was still reluctant to make such a commitment, concerned that she knew nothing about music and wouldn't be a help to Lawrence in his career. But Lawrence had the perfect answer to that argument. He didn't want her help in business. That was his department. He wanted a wife who would take care of his home and family, and create the kind of warm haven his own mother always had provided. And that's the way it has always been for the Welks.

They were married at 5:30 A.M. on April 19, 1931, at the Sacred Heart Cathedral in Sioux Falls. If the hour was unusual, so was the rest of the wedding day. Lawrence was on his way from an engagement in Nebraska to his next tour date in Wisconsin, and Sioux Falls was somewhere in the middle. There was no champagne wedding breakfast for the newlyweds: just coffee and donuts, then into the car and on the road. It was a pattern that was to be repeated often in their first few years as husband and wife. If Fern had any second thoughts about the marriage, they were not about Lawrence but about giving up her career. They were soon forgotten in the hectic atmosphere of life on the road, and Fern has never been sorry.

Like her husband, Fern was raised on a farm in St. Anthony,

Additional orchestra members and more formal stage settings became necessary as the group became more famous.

North Dakota. She was the second youngest of eight children (Lawrence was the third youngest of eight). Her family also came from Alsace-Lorraine, and were homesteaders as well. Her strict German-Catholic upbringing, almost exactly like Lawrence's, taught her to respect and obey her parents, and although she was always a dreamer, help with the chores came before anything else. Her father died from a ruptured appendix and peritonitis (Lawrence had been far luckier) when Fern was only three, and her mother, whose German and French heritage gave her the strength and resiliancy to carry on, took over running the farm and the family. It was not an easy life, although the Renners were not nearly as poor as the Welks were. When her mother was stricken with a gall bladder attack, and the nearest doctor was miles away, it was Fern who nursed her through the illness. It was then she knew she wanted to be a nurse. With her mother's blessings she began her studies at a boarding school run by Catholic nuns.

Life on the road was not easy for either Fern or Lawrence, although he was more or less used to it. For Fern, it was a completely different way of life, and although, in the beginning, she went everywhere with Lawrence, she soon began to dislike the constant traveling. They spent one or two days in a town and then were off to the next one, often driving all night. Sometimes, the accommodations were simply terrible and Fern would have a good cry. Then she would get up and try to make a home whatever the conditions. She always succeeded in adding just a bit of brightness to often gloomy rooms, and making them pleasant for Lawrence.

From Wisconsin, just after their wedding, they went to Chicago, but there was little work. So it was back to Yankton, where Lawrence set up a new tour schedule, and off to Dallas almost immediately. Dallas was a place of joy — and a near disaster. Fern announced that she was pregnant, and the band announced to Lawrence that they were leaving him. "You'll never make it to the big time," they said, "because you can't even speak English. And what's more," they told him, adding insult to injury, "you're keeping us from making it, too."

Lawrence was crushed. But his new responsibility as a prospective father, and his belief, that with God's help he could do anything, moved him into action. He went back to Yankton and hired a new band. Still known as the "Hotsy Totsy Boys," they went off on tour almost immediately; Lawrence was determined to prove that he could make it big. While they were on the road, Fern stayed in Dallas to be close to doctors she knew and trusted — and because she yearned to settle down in one place and to have a real home. Their first child, Shirley Jean, was born in Dallas on April 28, 1932. Lawrence was on the road at the time. When he finally got home, he promised Fern he'd at least try a more permanent way of life. They bought an old thirty-room hotel, and tried to make a go of it. It was re-named "The Lawrence" and they hoped it would become a second home for traveling musicians. It was an impossible task and turned out to be too much work for Fern. They had to give it up, but Lawrence was not defeated. He could always try again. Lawrence, his family, and his orchestra returned to Yankton and WNAX, but this time, Lawrence got himself a sponsor, the Honolulu Fruit Gum Company. He bought the gum in wholesale lots, had it rewrapped to his specifications, and sold it in ballrooms, drugstores, and restaurants wherever he was appearing. The "Hotsy Totsy Boys" had become "Lawrence Welk and His Honolulu Fruit Gum Orchestra." It was a successful venture, both musically and financially.

Bubbles in the Wine

onna Lee, the Welks' second daughter, was born on February 13, 1937; the little family had begun to grow. It was difficult for Fern, who was home alone with the children so much of the time. She had never been able to get adjusted to life on the road, and chose to carve a home base for her family while Lawrence toured. She had never liked going to the ballrooms where Lawrence played. The lack of privacy, the bright lights, and the crowds were not for her. She couldn't even dance with her own husband because part of Lawrence's appeal was his dancing with the women in the audience, who eagerly lined up for a whirl around the dance floor with him. He and the members of the band spent almost as much time dancing as they did playing, and the ladies loved it. Fern, secure in the knowledge that Lawrence would be coming home to her each evening, stayed happily with the children. It was often lonesome, and occasionally a handful, but somehow it was never really a big disappointment. She still goes with Lawrence only on very special occasions, like his yearly appearance at Lake Tahoe, where they stay in a mansionlike guest house with all the privacy Fern could ever hope for.

The band was booked into Pittsburgh's William Penn Hotel for New Year's Eve 1938, and with the engagement came a radio commitment for twenty broadcasts a week on the Mutual network, during the length of the appearance. For the first time, Lawrence and his band could be heard coast-to-coast. It was exciting, and that extra sparkle was transmitted right across the airwaves. His fans began bombarding the stations with mail, enthusiastically calling the music "bubbly," "sparkling," "effervescent," "never flat." It was all champagne to his ears, and "Lawrence Welk and His Champagne Music Makers" was born. It was a major turning point in his career, heralding a new name and style for the band. At last, Lawrence had a real identity as a musician, one that he would be known by for a lifetime.

The song Lawrence originally wrote to celebrate Shirley's birth, "You're My Home Sweet Home," was jazzed up from the original ballad to the frothy, upbeat tune, renamed — in a contest — "Bubbles in the Wine," and it became the Welk theme song. To carry the champagne theme even further, Lawrence's female vocalists became known as "Champagne Ladies." At the beginning of each performance, he would "turn on the bubble machine," make the sound of a champagne cork popping, and bring down his baton with the familiar, "A-one. . . ." The total effect was fantastic, and it has not, in the forty years since, lost one bit of its appeal to his fans.

According to Lawrence, the light, bubbly champagne sound of his music came about accidentally. He couldn't afford to hire good pick-up musicians — players who would just fill in for the length of the engagement — in fact, some of the musicians he could afford could hardly play at all. So all the arrangements were designed to be short and sweet, with no notes that had to be held too long. Voilà! The bubbly, champagne sounds that were to become his trademark.

The year 1940 was to be another exciting one for the Welks. Their first son, Lawrence Leroy Welk, Jr., was born in March, to much fanfare and celebration, and the Champagne Music Makers were booked for their first long-term engagement at the prestigious Trianon Ballroom in Chicago. It was one of the finest in the Midwest, and the realization of a long-time dream of Lawrence's — to play Chicago in a top

Right: This picture was taken when Welk was playing for soldiers and civilians all over the country during the war years.

(Memory Shop)

Lawrence Welk, Jr. was born in 1940, and Lawrence always hoped that his young offspring would take to the accordion as enthusiastically as he had. He bought Junior a toy instrument when he was just a tot, but Larry never was really interested in playing the accordion seriously. He works for his dad, now, but not in a musical capacity.

house. What started out as a twelve-week booking turned into nine years of steady employment at the Trianon, and its sister ballroom, the Aragon. Finally, Fern and the children had a real home base. The Welks moved into a house of their own and became a real family at last.

Life was good, except for one major drawback. Lawrence and the band were getting paid $1,750 a week when they first started at the Trianon. Nine years later, despite all protests, they were still getting $1,750 a week. Lawrence and the boys started feeling the pinch in the post-war economy. But their unhappiness was not just financial, although that was certainly a contributing factor. During the war years, they were allowed time off — or gave up their free days — to entertain the troops at USO dances, army bases, and veterans hospi-

tals. It was Lawrence's way of saying "thank you" to the country that had been so very good to him all these years. But now they felt a bit trapped by their six-nights-a-week performance schedule, which left them very little time for anything else.

The big break came in 1949. Lawrence convinced Miller High Life, "The Champagne of Bottled Beer," that it would be a natural for them to sponsor the Champagne Music Makers on a network radio show. It was a happy agreement that lasted two years. The band had their music stands redesigned to look like champagne buckets. Whenever the band went on tour, the Miller logo was prominently displayed and Lawrence never played in a hotel or dance hall that didn't sell Miller High Life.

No matter how busy he was, Lawrence always found time to spend with his daughters, Shirley and Donna.

When Shirley went off to college, everybody got into the act to help her pack — Mom, Dad, and even little brother.

Ping-pong is not everybody's game, but not only is it a way to relax for the Welks, but it makes spending time together fun. Shirley and Larry Jr. were the family champs.

Television

The Miller tour schedule took the orchestra to the West Coast in 1951, and Lawrence discovered television. An appearance on KTLA-TV in Los Angeles to promote a local appearance at the Aragon Ballroom in Santa Monica brought terrific viewer response. The audience loved the music and the music makers. KTLA signed Lawrence and his orchestra to a six-month contract. Their TV appearances had outdrawn all the network competition, and the Aragon was turning away business. Lawrence moved his family out to California, although Fern was reluctant to make the move. She liked Chicago, and not even the promise of beautiful sunny skies was appealing — until she got there. It turned out to be the last major move the Welk family had to make, and Fern took to southern California as easily as the public was taking to her husband.

The very idea of doing a TV show scared Lawrence half to death. He was, even after all these years, still uncomfortable speaking more than a few words at a time, and doing it on camera, in front of all those people, made his knees shake. Although he no longer panicked, or let other announcers talk

Left: Lawrence Welk has grown proportionately more handsome with his maturity as a performer. He's not quite the heart throb he was, but he still dazzles the ladies.

Fern always kept her public appearances to a minimum, but every once in a while some special occasion would tempt her to go out on the town with her famous husband.

For many years, Lawrence has been the Grand Marshal of the New Year's Day Rose Bowl Parade. It's an honor he looks forward to and loves.

for him, or even made such obvious mistakes as calling a microphone a microscope, it was still such a difficult chore for him. Even with cue cards, he kept his announcements down to a minimum. He still does. Lawrence loves to tell the story of the band's being offered $1,750 a week back in the thirties to appear in Milwaukee. The only catch was that he had to act as emcee. Lawrence turned it down because he was embarrassed by his accent. The theater manager wanted the band so much, he upped the offer. "For $3,500," Lawrence said, "I'll talk."

Lawrence could have spoken in any language. It didn't seem to matter, either in the ballroom or on TV. The audience loved him, and loved the music, which was language

One of Lawrence's biggest pleasures was coaching and sponsoring a Little League team. He's always loved kids and sports. Above right: Even the little ones love to dance with Lawrence, and he's not one to pass up an opportunity to polka with a pretty girl.

enough, and he spent four happy years on KTLA-TV.

During those years, Lawrence met producer Don Fedderson, who was an avid fan, and with his able assistance, convinced Dodge to sponsor the "Lawrence Welk Show" in a summer replacement spot on national television. It was just the beginning of a sixteen-year relationship with ABC-TV. When the show debuted on July 2, 1955, the reviews were mixed, and the first week's ratings were unimpressive. Lawrence was worried, and worked harder as the weeks went by. By the end of the summer, Welk, Dodge, and ABC knew they had a winner.

Golf is Lawrence's biggest love, second only to music and his family. He is out on the golf course as much as possible, with friends of many years. He says his lowest score was 79, and has an 18 handicap.

The charm and appeal of the early TV shows, and indeed, of Lawrence's current ones as well, lay in the fact that they were not like TV shows at all. They were like personal appearances in ballrooms, dance halls, and big hotel nightspots. There were no camera tricks, no special effects — just Lawrence and his musical family, and of course, the music.

What Lawrence Welk did was to take the standard formula for the typical orchestra leader and throw it out the window. The glamour-boy image, with fancy flashy clothes and a matching lifestyle, together with the kind of music understandable only to an elite few was — and still is — not for

In 1958, Ralph Edwards surprised Lawrence on "This Is Your Life." He was an easy guest to fool on the show – he thought he was going to the studio to make some commercials, and even had learned his lines perfectly. He was almost angry when it turned out to be a ruse.

Right: Lawrence and his family are camera-shy, but here's a fairly recent picture of him with Fern, their daughters, and their grandchildren. Shirley and her husband, Robert Fredericks, are the parents of Laura, Robert, David, and Jonathan. Donna Lee and James Mack's son is named Jimmy.

him. Instead, his viewers saw a handsome, fatherly man, simply dressed and totally unpretentious, who played the kind of music that could be danced to and enjoyed by everyone. The melody and the beat were instantly recognizable by young and old.

At a time when the dance-hall business in the United States was taking a nose dive into oblivion, Lawrence Welk brought the dance hall into the homes of 30 million people each week. He performed on TV almost exactly as he had done on tour for the past twenty-five years, by dancing with the ladies in the audience, announcing special events, and holding polka or waltz contests. He was totally himself. He never changed his style for television; he merely increased his viewing public.

Lawrence's feelings about why his show became so popular are based on two concepts he has never given up: nice, simple, "danceable" music, and his "musical family," made up of nice people who like each other, like working with each other, and can transmit that friendliness on TV. He has always felt that he would rather have a performer stay home than appear with a troubled look on his face. It would upset his fans too much, and the happiness of his fans is what has always been most important to Lawrence.

Over the years, he has built his musical family into a trademark as easily recognized as the bubble machine or his own exclamations of "wunnerful, wunnerful!" A collection of beautiful women who are talented, sincere, and obviously adore working with each other and with Lawrence have become "America's Sweethearts" with followings all their own. The men in the "family" are clean-cut and unaffected and each one reminds Welk's viewers of the "boy next door."

It was, in 1955, a fresh and unique style that immediately captured the hearts of the young and old. In his sixteen years with ABC, Lawrence continued to build his "family," his wholesome presentation, and his loyal, unswerving following. By 1971, he had, still, one of the top ten shows on television, and 30 million fans who eagerly turned their dials to the "Lawrence Welk Show" each week.

Canceled!

Even with all this, ABC felt that the Welk show was not reaching the younger, more affluent audiences. Despite its popularity with older viewers, and without so much as a discussion with its star, they canceled the show. Lawrence, however, had known that something was brewing. ABC had been avoiding talking renewal with him and his advisers, but nothing had been decided. He was on the golf course when it happened, and was called to the phone. On the other end was a wire-service reporter asking him how he felt — ABC had not even taken the time to notify him properly. To say that Lawrence was disappointed would be an understatement. He was heartbroken, worrying about his musical family and his fans. What would they do?

Only one person was truly pleased with the idea of an unemployed Lawrence Welk — his wife. She hoped this might be the time when he would retire. After all, he was sixty-eight years old, and had been working steadily for the past forty-seven of them. Yet, deep in her heart, she knew he wouldn't stop now. Not only was music his life and breath, but he had a very genuine concern for all the people who

Left: As Lawrence and his orchestra became more and more popular, he was able to relax a little, especially in front of the photographers.

depended on him for a living. Deep down, Lawrence also knew he wouldn't retire. He had considered it briefly when his sixty-fifth birthday approached, but he didn't feel there was anyone to whom he could really trust the care and control of his musical family.

If Lawrence was surprised and disconsolate, his fans were furious. A literal avalanche of mail and calls protesting the cancellation of the show arrived at ABC, Lawrence's offices, and the FCC. It didn't change the network's mind, but Lawrence began fighting his battle for survival. He began by making sure his performers were taken care of. He had, years before, put into effect a profit-sharing plan. But he was worried that all his people, with their families to support, wouldn't be able to stretch it too far or for too long. So, he set up an ambitious tour schedule to allow his "family" to get lots of public exposure to help them through the times when they wouldn't be appearing on TV. He even booked them into Madison Square Garden, a potential disaster since the sophisticated New York audiences were not the usual Welk fans. He turned it into a dramatic triumph — not one single seat in the house was empty!

But this was not all Lawrence was doing. He and Don Fedderson had read the enormous support from the fans as a sign to go out and do something unprecedented. They would form a syndicated network themselves, and sell the "Lawrence Welk Show" independently. It took just three months to sign up the first 207 stations — independents, network affiliates, and UHF channels. These 207 stations (many of them ABC affiliates) represented 55 million homes. Within a year, Lawrence was reaching a larger audience than he had with ABC. In the first six years of syndication, more than 7.1 billion people watched the show. Today, over 265 stations carry the "Lawrence Welk Show." The transition from network to syndication was so smooth that Lawrence and company did not miss a single week, and hardly anyone noticed there had been a change. ABC showed re-runs throughout the summer, and by September, Lawrence's first syndicated show was on the air. He has been on national television for twenty-three years without a break — and he shows no signs of letting up.

The Man and the Myth

He appears to be a man of great sensitivity, understanding and gentleness; a paternal figure whose major concern is the well-being of his family. That is certainly the side of Lawrence Welk best known to his fans. But he has other strengths, paternalistic in nature, as well, that he exercises more cautiously and mostly with his "musical family."

His temper has always given him trouble, especially when he feels his trust has been betrayed. He may speak softly, or remain rather quiet, but when he's angry, his eyes spit fire, and it's hard to conceal. Lawrence has learned to control his temper a great deal, mostly with the help of a church pamphlet titled "How to Check Your Anger" which taught him to keep his pride from running away with him. But, his temper can flash dangerously when he thinks his musicians are not putting in enough hours of practice to keep the orchestra running smoothly, or when his singers and dancers are rehearsing without the definite precision he demands. By nature, he is a perfectionist and expects perfection from everyone else. He has no use for lazy, indifferent performers, and since he puts all his energy into each show, he feels that anything less than total commitment and concentration is not good enough.

He has, because of his constant quest for the perfect performance, been called tyrannical with his musical family; the classic Teutonic father figure, autocratic and inflexible. And some of his "rules" are indeed inflexible. Foremost is the music. He insists on playing only what his audiences have told him, over the years, they want to hear, and won't even consider music he himself doesn't understand. If a song has a double meaning, dirty words, or suggests or condones anything immoral, you won't hear it on the "Lawrence Welk Show." He thinks young, he says, and listens to "middle-of-the-road" rock music, but every song up for consideration is very carefully analyzed before it's accepted. His attitude explains why "Raindrops Keep Fallin' on My Head" or "You Light up My Life" are about as avant garde as you can expect.

Other rules are much more personal. There is no smoking or drinking during rehearsals or performances; no frowning faces on camera; no cleavage or otherwise revealing costumes for the women, and no divorces or scandals if at all avoidable. Lawrence is not above getting involved in his performers' personal lives to mediate in domestic quarrels — even if only to guarantee that on camera, or before an audience, everyone looks happy. He claims it's merely his way of being fatherly and protective.

Music, to Lawrence, is a way of showing the solidarity of the kind of family life he holds so dear, so it's no wonder the members of his band must be as acceptable to him as members of his own family. If the methods seem harsh, it's only because he feels he must enforce certain standards to bring this image across. And in very large measure, he has been successful. The family wholesomeness the show projects is one of the things that has kept his fans coming back for more.

If Lawrence himself admits to any one big weakness, it's his attitude towards money. Some people call him cheap; he says he's thrifty, or sensible. It stems, of course, from all those early, hungry years, when thrift was not a choice but a necessity. He firmly believes that money should be earned by hard work, and that philosophy is reflected in the way he pays his own musicians and performers. With few excep-

tions, they all receive union scale. All protests are met with a simple explanation: his performers all have steady jobs, lots of exposure, good opportunities to freelance, and a handsome profit-sharing plan. They also have no contracts. If anyone doesn't like the system, he can always leave. Several have, for just that reason, but many more have stayed with Lawrence for great lengths of time.

On a rare occasion in public, Fern and Lawrence attended the Bob Hope–USO Tribute to Gerald Ford in December 1977.

The Plan

Lawrence Welk says he has had six major goals to accomplish in his seventy-five years. The first was to grow big enough to reach the pedals on the family pump organ. The second was to own an accordion. Third was to get off the farm and into a musical career. Fourth was to have his own band; fifth was to appear on radio and join the Big Band league. Last was to have a TV show of his own. He has realized each of his goals, despite all the hardships and difficulties along the way. Very thankful for the opportunities he found along the road to success, he has put great emphasis on helping others — especially the members of his musical family — to realize their goals.

The maestro is quick to admit he is a better showman and businessman than he is a musician. He never could read music well, but he loves leading his orchestra more than anything. He's a bit rueful that his accordion playing is not what it could be, since he has less time to practice now than he ever did. This explains, to some extent, why he insists on practice from his musicians, and has made preparedness an essential requisite for his "plan."

Left: A portrait of Lawrence in a smiling but pensive mood. The ring he wears is one he bought in the early thirties with his first big paycheck. It was a symbol to him of success.

As Lawrence envisions it, the "plan" is a basic sharing of experience, knowledge, friendship, and dreams — and, of course, profits. Just like in any family, success is based on love and understanding. Lawrence is the father who helps his fifty children realize their dreams. They, in turn, try their best to make him proud of them, and are well rewarded for their efforts.

Because the Welk performers have no contracts, Lawrence feels they stay with him because they want to, and because they have the freedom to develop their talents, as well as their trust and confidence in each other. To bolster that trust and confidence, to build humanity to its highest degree, Lawrence's overall plan revolves around a five-fold sharing system that motivates, builds character, creates happiness, and in the long run, is better business. The social, moral, educational, and emotional aspects of the sharing system can't really be measured accurately, but the financial sharing can. It's a deceptively simple idea: the members contribute their talent and dedication; the organization contributes money; and up to 15 percent of each individual's earnings each year is invested for him. The longer anyone stays, the bigger his potential income gets. There are merit bonuses, too, for jobs especially well done. They may be money, gifts, or more responsibility, depending on the individual, and what Lawrence thinks he or she needs most.

In return, Lawrence asks that his musical family follow his list of "Golden Rules" (in addition to whatever specific directions he gives them): that they always be on time, and prepared for what they are about to do; that they be honest and truthful at all times; that they work hard, learn humility, and give freely of themselves; that they take direction, but also show initiative where possible; and that they present a clean and wholesome image, both onstage and off.

For youngsters who come into the Welk fold, Lawrence has developed the "Youth Opportunity Plan," that has two basic parts, the first being on-the-job training. Lawrence likes to put young performers in the hands of his more experienced people and expects them to teach the newcomers the ropes. This is usually a one-year apprenticeship, with the youngsters getting paid all the while, and assimilating the techniques and attitudes that will turn them into professionals. The other half of the plan is much more subtle. Lawrence calls it "personality and character training." By associating with the seasoned members of the musical family, Lawrence hopes his potential stars will learn from their examples what is expected of them, and how to go about developing similar attitudes.

There have been successes and failures with both plans. But the most important thing, to Lawrence, in any case, is that he has given people opportunity to develop. He offers as much help as he can, but ultimately, the final result is up to the individual.

This past January Lawrence was part of a famous foursome at the thirty-seventh Crosby Pro-Am Golf Tournament at Pebble Beach. His unlikely partner was singer Jim Seals, of Seals and Crofts, whose music is as different from Lawrence's as the difference in their ages.

(Wide World Photos)

The Welk Organization

Harking back to his philosophy that money has to be earned to be deserved, Lawrence sets a prime example. He has no idea, he says, nor does he care, just how much he's worth. But the lettering on his office door tells you a little something: Teleklew Productions; Lawrence Welk Offices; Champagne Music Corporation; Lawrence Welk Foundation. There's more than bubbles behind it. The office is in the Lawrence Welk Union Bank Building, a $3.5 million structure built in 1961. He also owns an interest in Wilshire West, a $16 million office and apartment complex. Among his other enterprises are the Lawrence Welk Country Club Estates, a mobile home retirement village in Escondido, complete with its own golf course, swimming pool, restaurant, and motel. Lawrence is chairman and president of Teleklew, which not only produces his TV show, but oversees the personal appearances of the "family" members. He holds the rights to more than 4,600 songs (among them, all the works of Jerome Kern), having acquired sixteen music publishing companies over the years. There are, of course, also the royalties from record albums, concert revenues, and sales of souvenir items.

Lawrence is no longer the poor farm boy, scratching out a bare living with his mail-order accordion, but a wealthy, respected figure, with little that he does not open to public scrutiny. Yet his concept of family is so important to him, that he tries, though not always successfully, to keep his private life separate and apart from his public one. He and Fern live in a magnificent $500,000 ranch-style house overlooking the Pacific Palisades. It is sort of a "repayment" to Fern for all the years spent on the road or in rented apartments and other people's houses. Spacious and warm, the house is always open to their three children and ten grandchildren.

Lawrence follows a daily regime that would wear out a much younger man. He's usually up by 5:30 A.M. for a little practice on the old golf swing. Then it's a half-hour swim in his heated pool, a long, relaxing shower, and breakfast with Fern. He's usually in his office by 8:00 A.M. Before returning home, he might get in a few holes of golf, and if they have no special plans, he and Fern will have a simple dinner and watch some TV. Their favorite show, naturally, is the "Lawrence Welk Show." They not only watch it, they even dance to the music. Lawrence's favorite room in the glass and stone house is the music room, where he can stretch out in his favorite easy chair and read, or play the organ. Fern will often go to sleep earlier than her husband, who likes to sit up and read the Bible before bed. Lawrence's deep faith, and Fern's as well, is one of their secrets for a long and happy marriage.

They have come a long way over the years, but they are still simple folks, and that's the way they like it.

The Champagne Ladies

More than just the man himself, the Lawrence Welk legend is built, in good measure, around the people who surround him, support him, and bolster his image of *paterfamilias*. Some fifty hard-working, talented, and well-loved performers make up Lawrence's musical family. His perfectionist nature demands, however, that they be of a very specific character and moral fiber, as well as extremely talented.

Perhaps no other performers have so personified Lawrence's ideals as his "Champagne Ladies" — attractive (even beautiful), talented (of course), from a solid family background, and with strong religious and life values, which are perhaps not as stringent, but certainly compatible with his own. From the first, even before there was anything officially called "Champagne Music," his female vocalists were virtuous, upright young women, who offered his audiences the embodiment of the ideal woman.

In the almost forty years since the first official "Champagne Lady," seven lovely women have held that title. But it really

all began before anyone had ever thought to make the connection between Lawrence's musical style and champagne. Maxine Grey, a winsome Southern belle from New Orleans, was the first permanent vocalist with the band. Although not officially a "Champagne Lady," she set the pattern for the future. Fern actually discovered her, one day, singing on a radio broadcast in Dallas, and convinced Lawrence to hire her. It was one of the few times Fern ever advised her husband about anything musical, and her judgment proved to be a good one. Maxine had a bright smile and charming drawl that charmed people from all over. When she left the Welk band in 1936 to sing with Hal Kemp's Orchestra, Lawrence had a hard time finding a replacement as popular with the audiences as she had been. A variety of female singers had to be hired to fill the gap.

Along with the new name, the "Champagne Music Makers," came the idea to call the featured singer the "Champagne Lady," and the first to hold this title officially was Lois Best. Lawrence had first heard her sing with the Benny Burton Orchestra and finally hired her, a few years later in 1939, when she and the band were in Boston. Lois was a vivacious dark-haired beauty, full of life and love, and it didn't take long for her to fall head over heels for Jules Herman, a trumpet player in the band. They were married, and in 1940, Lois left to be a full-time wife. Although proud of his role as a matchmaker, Lawrence was still pretty strict about romances among the members of his group, and while he admired Lois's talents, she probably would not have been allowed to continue with the band.

Lois's successor was Jayne Walton, a "Champagne Lady" of surprising versatility. She was as American as apple pie, but her mixed background — her family was Irish, but she was born in Mexico and lived there with her parents until she was eight — lent an international flavor to the show that the audience responded to instantly. She spoke fluent Spanish, and her romantic versions of Spanish ballads were what first caught Lawrence's attention. He heard her on the radio, over Omaha's WOW, and her rendition of "Maria Elena" became both a Welk and an audience favorite. Love intervened, though, and she left to get married in 1945.

Jayne's departure paved the way for sparkling seventeen-year-old Joan Mowery, another in Lawrence's long line of

Left: Alice Lon was a very special "Champagne Lady," the first to be on national TV when Lawrence's show went on the air.

Above: The first official "Champagne Lady" with the orchestra was dark-eyed Lois Best. She joined in 1939, and stayed for a little over a year. Above right: Jayne Walton was the second "Champagne Lady." She wowed the audiences with her haunting Spanish ballads, especially "Maria Elena."

beautiful brunettes. For two years, her romantic duets with Bob Cromer stopped the show. Joan also had a natural flair for comedy which she demonstrated in the best theatrical tradition with her countrified version of "Doin' What Comes Naturally." She fondly said of her years with the band, "I owe a lot to Lawrence. He teaches a lesson that continues through life . . . always give more than you hope to receive."

The fourth Champagne Lady was Helen Ramsay, a petite young woman with a sweet, strong voice. She was a favorite at the Trianon Ballroom in Chicago, and gave a special magic to such old standards as "Blue Moon" and "It Might As Well Be Spring."

It was Roberta Linn, the next of the dark-haired "Champagne Ladies," who went with Lawrence to California in 1951. She was so popular with both the audiences and the band,

that there was no question of her being a featured performer at the Aragon Ballroom. Her special strength, besides, of course, her delightful voice and pretty face, was her infectious giggle which soon had everyone giggling right along with her. She says of her former boss, "Lawrence is marvelous with people. He loves to be where there's an audience."

When Roberta left she was replaced by Alice Lon, the lady whose delicious smile and swirling petticoats — handmade by her mother from yards and yards of net and tulle — made her the darling of TV audiences from coast-to-coast. She was the first TV "Champagne Lady," the woman who, when she danced a polka with Lawrence, was the envy of millions of women across the country. For the premiere show, Alice sang "Love Me or Leave Me" with such feeling and emotion that she had everyone in tears.

Above: Helen Ramsay had a sultry look, but she was a sweet young girl with a lovely voice. She was a favorite with everyone in the band and in the audience. Above left: The third dark-eyed brunette "Champagne Lady" was Joan Mowery. She was only seventeen when she started out with Lawrence, and he thought of her as a daughter.

Above: For Roberta Linn, being "Champagne Lady" meant a chance to go to California with the band in 1951. She was a big hit with Lawrence at the Aragon Ballroom. Above right: Alice Lon and Dick Dale.

Right: The premiere show was particularly memorable. Alice sang "Love Me or Leave Me," and the finale was a duet with Jimmie Rogers. Behind Alice, Jimmy, and Lawrence, you can pick out Myron Floren and Dick Dale.

Alice was no stranger to performing. She sang, danced, and played the piano almost as soon as she could talk. Her family was a musical one, and they encouraged her to do her first radio show when she was six. By the time she was ten, she had her own weekly program. In college, Alice joined theatre and musical groups, touring with them during semester breaks, but her first really big opportunity came when she was chosen to be the feature singer on Don McNeill's "Breakfast Club" in Chicago. She stayed with Lawrence for six years, and then decided to try it as a single.

The parting was not a pleasant one. Alice was supporting three young sons, and one of the things she complained about was that she was not making enough money. The other real argument, though, was actually over just what kind of

Romantic duets were a specialty for Alice Lon. Here she sings with Jimmie Rogers.

songs Alice felt she should be singing. She ran up against Lawrence's very strong feelings about what was right for his show, and after a year of bitter arguments, she left, saying, "I just couldn't take it any more. Lawrence has changed. It isn't the same happy family it used to be when I joined. Lawrence is just so hard to work for now; he lacks consideration and there are no exceptions in his book."

Lawrence's reaction to Alice's farewell was cool. He called her "a peach of a girl," but said he felt she had been badly advised. Had she come to him to talk it over, he said, everything could have been straightened out in a friendly way. The audience deeply felt the split in the Welk family, and everyone had an opinion about it. The fan mail was unbelievable!

It took two years and a succession of short-lived vocalists

Left: The accordion of flowers was a special gift to Lawrence and the members of the show from friends and fans.

(Memory Shop)

Left: Norma Zimmer broke the pattern of "Champagne Ladies" when she became number seven in 1961. She was the first blonde to hold the title, and she's been with Lawrence for seventeen years.

Above: The "Gay Nineties" era is a perfect one for Norma. She loves the costumes, and the kinds of songs she gets to sing while wearing them. A rollicking polka, left, with her boss is an audience favorite as well as a Zimmer and Welk favorite.

before Lawrence found his next and reigning "Champagne Lady," Norma Zimmer. It was well worth the wait. She is one of the most popular performers on the show, and her natural warmth and friendliness has built her a fan population all her own. She is equally as popular with the rest of the Welk family for she radiates such happiness and good feelings. Everyone is immediately caught up in her presence. She is a charming, natural lady with whom the audience readily identifies, and who is as easily recognized as Lawrence Welk himself.

The real key to Norma's happiness is her marriage to Randy Zimmer, and their two grown sons. They've been married for more than thirty years, and have found the perfect blend of togetherness and separate identities.

Norma actually first sang with Lawrence in 1959, and then made several guest appearances throughout 1960. On the New Year's Eve Show, he asked her to become a permanent member of the family, and in August 1961, Lawrence officially crowned her "Champagne Lady" number seven. Norma is the only one of them all, right back to the original prototype, Maxine Grey, who is a blonde — maybe it's part of what makes her so special.

What also sets her apart from her predecessors are the convictions she shares with Lawrence, strong devotion to religion, and belief in the sacred nature of the family. Norma is dedicated to the Billy Graham crusade, and it's one of the few outside activities in which she participates. All the rest of her spare time is spent with her husband and sons, and Lawrence approves heartily. She is one of the few exceptions to his rule that all members of his troupe must tour with him in the summer. He knows that if Norma was ever forced to choose between traveling and her family, he would lose in the end.

Norma is so well-liked and appreciated by the rest of the "family," that no one minds that she has special privileges. Tanya Falan holds her up as an idol, and would like to be just like her; several male members of the show have often mused, . . ." If I weren't happily married, I would propose to Norma."

She is indeed a very special lady.

Right: As you can see, Lawrence is a man of many talents. He serenaded Norma with the uke in a special Hawaiian segment of the show.

Those Who Left

Right: Lawrence didn't just sing with his girls; he helped them with their studies and school-work, and with their religious training. Their devout Catholicism, like Lawrence's own, saw them through troubles as well as good times.

Of all the personalities that have ever been with Lawrence Welk, undeniably the most popular have been the Lennon Sisters. Thirty million people watched them grow up in front of their eyes, and thirty million people cried when they heard the Lennons had left Lawrence for other, perhaps greener, pastures. No other Welk stars have been talked about as much, or been missed as much since. No other Welk stars have given a generation of grandmothers so much to hope for in their own families.

It was Christmas Eve 1955 when Lawrence introduced Dianne, Peggy, Kathy, and Janet Lennon — then, respectively, sixteen, fourteen, twelve, and nine — to his viewers. They were an instant smash, and a month later, became permanent members of the Welk family. When they left, after twelve years, everyone was shocked. Why had they gone? What happened? As abrupt as their departure might have seemed, it had actually been brewing behind the scenes for some time.

The Lennons were discovered by Lawrence Welk, Jr., who went to high school with Dianne. He had heard the sisters

(Memory Shop)

perform at school shows and church functions, and insisted that his dad listen to them. Larry Jr. brought them over to sing a couple of tunes for his father who at the time was recovering from the flu. They made him feel so much better, that he got right on the phone with his agent and put them on his show.

They became like daughters to him, both on camera and off. They couldn't read music and had never had a singing lesson, but Lawrence took them under his wing. Everybody in the musical family helped develop their natural talent. They were universally adored, and their progress, from cute, talented little girls to beautiful young women was avidly fol-

When the Lennon Sisters first appeared with Lawrence in 1955, they were an instant smash. Left to right: Dianne, Janet, Lawrence, Peggy, and Kathy.

lowed by the public. Their boyfriends, their marriages, and the birth of their children, made magazine headlines; but nothing added more grist to the gossip mill than their departure from the "Lawrence Welk Show."

Lawrence believes that the first real inkling that their relationship was changing came in 1960, when Dianne left to get married. It was a sad time for Lawrence, but a joyous one, too. She left with his blessing. Peggy, Kathy, and Janet continued on as a trio until Dianne rejoined them in 1964. Lawrence welcomed her back with open arms. By this time, though, all the sisters were married, and beginning to have families of their own. Their places in the Welk family, onstage and off, were beginning to take different shapes.

By 1968, it became obvious to Lawrence, at least, that the Lennons were restless and dissatisfied. He blames their decision to leave the show on bad advice from agents who promised them the stars if they would just go out on their own. They wanted to cut down their work schedule with Lawrence, and just appear on TV with him once a month. And, they asked to be excused from touring with the rest of the band during the summer. This was intolerable to Lawrence. He absolutely could not make exceptions to his rule that all the stars of the "Lawrence Welk Show" appear on every TV broadcast, and at every club and concert date as well. He tried desperately to find a workable compromise, as he had done a few times in the past, even though it was against his rules, but he couldn't. Lawrence was unmovable; the Lennons determined to have every opportunity available to develop their nightclub act. So they left, packing in twelve years of fond and happy memories with their costumes as they emptied their dressing rooms.

Of all the flaps concerning the "Lawrence Welk Show," this one hit the hardest. Everyone was involved — the press, the gossip columnists, the public relations offices. And the public could just not get enough information.

It would be foolish to think for a minute that Lawrence was not hurt by their leaving. He was, and very deeply. Not so much that they quit, but by the very fact that they wanted to. He felt, after all, like a second father to them, and every sensational, but mistaken, version of why and how they left him hurt a little more.

But maybe the rift wasn't as large as the press made it out to be, for, alternatively, it did begin to heal. When the sisters' dear father, Bill Lennon, was brutally and inexplicably gunned down in broad daylight, about a year after the Lennons had left the show, Lawrence and Fern were there to offer comfort and consolation. When Lawrence's son, Larry Jr. married Tanya Falan in 1970, the girls were at the wedding to help the Welks celebrate. When the Lennon Sisters and Jimmy Durante teamed up for a weekly TV show, Lawrence gave them all the help he could to help boost their sinking ratings. Unfortunately, even he couldn't help them. That show, and their subsequent nightclub act, comprised a startling departure from the kind of things they had done on Lawrence's shows. Perhaps the public wasn't quite ready for the transition from costumes that buttoned up to the neck and barely exposed a knee to the sexy, abbreviated outfits and real "show biz" arrangements that spiced up their new act.

On a recent TV show celebrating ABC's first fifty years — and the "Lawrence Welk Show" certainly played a large part in them — the Lennons looked sensational in their new act. So did Lawrence Welk. It was the first time they had been on the same stage in ten years.

Today, the Lennons are wives and mothers first, and entertainers only occasionally. Dianne, the oldest, is almost forty, and the mother of three children. When she married her high school sweetheart, Dick Gass, in 1960, she left the show. But when Peggy left to have a baby, Dianne filled in — and stayed.

Peggy was the workhorse of the group, and she never thought she'd have the time to get married. But she did, to Welk trumpet player Dick Cathcart, in 1964. They have six children. During the last six years the Lennons were with Lawrence, it seemed as if one or another of them was always pregnant. Costume designer Rose Weiss had a hard time figuring out different ways to hide impending motherhood, and the audience had a wonderful time guessing who was about to become a mother next.

The only one of the sisters with no children is Kathy. She married Mahlon Clark, a former lead saxophonist with the Welk orchestra. Because Mahlon was divorced, they couldn't be married in the Catholic church, and Kathy had a painful decision to make. Lawrence, in his role of protector and adviser to the girls, didn't feel he could advise Kathy. All he could do was wish her happiness and joy.

Janet was always the baby of the group, and millions of TV viewers still remember her best as the awkward little girl with the pigtails, ankle-length socks, and patent leather shoes. Today, she is a grown-up blonde, the mother of three, and wife to TV director Lee Bernhardi. Only the smile and her flashing eyes tell you it's the same little Janet who so shamelessly broke the hearts of her countless fans.

Lawrence saw the Lennon Sisters through a whole spectrum of joys and heartbreaks. He was always there when they needed him; always ready with a word of encouragement or praise. It broke his heart to see them go, and no other leave-takings have been nearly as painful for him.

Many others have left the Welk organization but with much less fanfare and far fewer years of memories than the Lennons. Some have gone by choice, others have had the decision taken out of their hands.

The most recent of Lawrence's "children" to break away and try her own wings left him doubly wounded. Not only was he losing one of his most popular female vocalists, but she was his very own daughter-in-law, Tanya, the mother of his namesake grandchild, Lawrence Welk III.

Although he tried valiantly not to show her any undue favoritism, Tanya Falan Welk very obviously had a special place in Lawrence's heart. When Mary Lee Schaeffer, president of the Welk Fan Club, first heard Tanya sing at Disneyland's World of Tomorrow, she knew this was a girl of special talents. Tanya first appeared on the New Year's Eve 1967 show, and the audience response was terrific. She was invited to become a regular.

Young, vivacious Tanya was in love at the time, with a singer that her parents heartily disapproved of. Though she said she was not ready to get married for at least five years, her whole life changed when she fell in love with Lawrence Welk, Jr. No one was more pleased than Lawrence himself when Tanya and Larry Jr. began dating, and the pride and joy with which he announced their wedding, in 1968, was contagious. When Tanya gave birth to Larry III, and then to their younger son, Kevin, it was hard to tell who was happier, Lawrence Jr. or Sr.

Last November, Tanya opened her nightclub act at Studio One Back Lot in Los Angeles and smartly announced that after being on the "Lawrence Welk Show" for ten years, she "was finally getting into show business." It was quite an announcement, subject to many levels of interpretation. Her husband thought the whole thing was quite funny, but Lawrence Sr. was not amused. It was a mutinous act in his eyes, and one that will be difficult to forgive or forget. Although he refused to comment about it for publication, it's a good bet he had quite a few words to offer in private.

A few years before, Natalie Nevins left with almost as much of a bang as Tanya. She was fired for not showing up for a Spokane, Washington concert date. Natalie had been with Lawrence since 1965, after auditioning for him over the tele-

Right: As the girls grew older and more sophisticated, they began to lead lives of their own. But to Lawrence, they were always "his" youngsters.

(Memory Shop)

phone. She sang, played the flute, and was a talented comedienne whom everyone adored. When she was fired, her fans and her friends were genuinely surprised. She said she had missed the performance because she was sick, but apparently forgot to tell anyone she wouldn't be there, and couldn't produce a doctor's note to verify her illness. Natalie tried to make amends, even baking Lawrence a dozen of her famous blueberry muffins, but he was not to be moved. Rules are rules, according to the Welk code, and are not meant to be broken.

Jazz clarinetist Pete Fountain left the Welk orchestra under somewhat of a cloud, too. He admitted that Lawrence was a hard taskmaster, and that there were, presumably, too many stylistic differences between them for him to stay on. Violinist Dick Kessner claimed he was going broke as a Champagne Music Maker. Popular Andra Willis, who was one of the original girls brought in as a replacement for the Lennons, was fired, or resigned, because she felt life with her husband was more important than touring and making personal appearances with the orchestra during the summer. Her parting with Lawrence was a friendly one, but it disappointed her fans greatly.

For some of Lawrence's ex-stars, marriage took precedence over career, and when wedding bells rang, they also played farewell to the show. Barbara Boylen, Bobby Burgess's first dancing partner, "retired" to marry Greg Dixon, who used to be a member of the "Blenders," a singing quartet that started in college and wound up on the Welk show. She had tripped the light fantastic with Bobby for six years before giving it all up for home and family. If her fans were disappointed, it was only because she and Bobby seemed like such a perfect couple on the screen, and they were surprised that they were not marrying each other.

Country-and-western singer Lynn Anderson was with Lawrence only a short time, but she was extremely popular and sorely missed. She left for two reasons: to be nearer to her husband, a music publisher whose work kept him in Nashville, and to pick up her own successful singing career again. She was already a "Country Singer of the Year" award winner, and her version of "I Never Promised You a Rose Garden" has become a classic.

Salli Flynn, the brunette half of the Sandi and Salli duo, also

Pete Fountain played the clarinet in Lawrence's orchestra for many years, and it gave him a good solid background when he went off on his own.

left to try a solo act. When she married Clay Hart, another former Welk musician, in 1974, she gave it all up for family life. Their romance started on the show, but it wasn't until after they had both gone on to other things that they finally tied the knot.

The bond between Lawrence and Jo Ann Castle was one of love and understanding. She had been with him for ten years, and Lawrence had stood by through the birth of a handicapped child, a divorce, and a new marriage. When she decided to leave the show, it was with tears, but with the knowledge that he knew and approved of her need to try to prove to the world that she was more than a honky-tonk ragtime pianist. She went with Lawrence's full support and blessings.

The Lennons gave up their "sugar-sweet" image when they left the Welk Show in 1968. Today they are mature, slick performers, who even do a mock striptease in their Las Vegas nightclub act. Left to right: Kathy, Janet, Dianne and Peggy.

Those Who Stayed

Over the years, although there have been many changes on the "Lawrence Welk Show," there is a certain continuity in the "family" that has existed since Lawrence's pre-TV days. Faces may have disappeared, and new ones taken their place, but the basic attitudes are not any different. The most popular, and most loved personalities are primary examples of this. They are almost as well known as Lawrence himself, and for much the same reasons: their sincerity, basic goodness, family image, and wholesomeness. Their personal triumphs — weddings, graduations, new babies, grandchildren — are regularly announced on the air as they happen. And Lawrence is every bit as excited about them as the fans are.

Everyone knows, for example, that if there's anyone who might conceivably take over Lawrence's job, should the indefatiguable Mr. Welk decide to retire, it would be Myron Floren. He's been with Lawrence for twenty-eight years, and you could say he'd be first in line if and when the baton is passed on. He's almost as indispensable to the Music Makers as Lawrence himself.

Right: One of the highlights of Lawrence's Christmas shows has been all the wives, husbands, and children of his "musical family." Even Fern makes an appearance, as do daughters Shirley and Donna along with their husbands and kids.

Myron almost didn't make it as a member of the band. His nimble-fingered accordion playing impressed Lawrence, but nearly everyone else thought that what the band needed least was another accordion player, especially one who played better than Lawrence himself. But Lawrence knew exactly who and what he wanted, and Myron was hired. He had actually first heard him in 1944, when Myron was a member of a hillbilly group called the "Buckeyes," but it was not a memorable meeting. Six years later, when Lawrence heard the group again, something clicked. This virtuoso of the "squeeze box" would be a valuable addition to the orchestra.

Like Lawrence, Myron fell in love with the accordion as a young boy, and sent away for his mail-order instrument when he was seven. He taught himself to play, but unlike Lawrence, who was too busy with his farm chores, Myron would practice as much as eight hours a day until he was good enough to play in public. He worked his way through college giving accordion lessons door-to-door. One of his best students, a pretty lass named Berdyne, became his wife. They have five daughters, all musically inclined, and when their second oldest, Kristie, married the Welk show's star dancer, Bobby Burgess, the wedding was a spectacular blending of musical families. Lawrence was there, of course; and almost as bursting with pride as the father of the bride himself.

If Bobby Burgess has a familiar face, it could be because at the age of fourteen he started a four-year stint as a Mouseketeer on the "Mickey Mouse Club." He started dancing when he was three years old, and all those years of practicing finally paid off. By the time he danced his way into Long Beach State College, he and his pretty partner, Barbara Boylen, were so good that they won Lawrence Welk's "Calcutta Dance Contest" in the spring of 1961. By August, the pair were regular members of the show, and immensely popular. When Bobby married Kristie Floren in 1971 — they first met when she was nine, but the romance took eight years to get serious — his fans went wild. They were only slightly disappointed that he hadn't married his current dancing partner, Cissy King, but they were delighted that Bobby chose to keep his family in the "family."

Arthur Duncan is another talented dancer on the show. He feels he owes so very much to Lawrence Welk. Arthur was one of the first black men to have a permanent spot on a TV variety show, and Lawrence was one of the first of the big stars to make that opportunity available. Arthur's dancing feet won him his permanent position over hundreds of other hoofers at a mass audition. Arthur was born and raised in Los Angeles and he has danced his way across continents — including a year as a featured performer on a Melbourne, Australia TV show. He and his wife Donna have been married for nearly twenty years, and are both avid tennis players and world travelers.

For Jack Imel, dancing is only one of his many accomplishments. But, when he, Arthur, and Bobby dance together on stage, there's magic in the air. When Jack joined the troupe, fresh out of the Navy in 1956, he dazzled Lawrence with an unusual display of his musical abilities — marimba, trumpet, drums, and vibraphone. If that wasn't enough, he could dance up a storm. He is also a valuable member of the production staff responsible for getting the Welk show on the air each week, which hardly leaves him enough time to spend with his wife, Norma, and their five children.

Jimmy Roberts, Ken Delo, and Joe Feeney sing their way into the hearts of millions of ladies every week, and have been doing it, happily, for years. There's nothing any of them enjoys more than crooning a romantic ballad to that very special woman in the audience. Joe, the Irish tenor with the magic voice, used to be a soprano as a boy in his church choir, and it was a priest who first brought him to Lawrence's attention. Joe, his wife Georgia, and their ten children, all play musical instruments, sing, or in some way follow in their father's musical footsteps.

Breaking the tradition of not having married couples perform together, Ralna English and Guy Hovis are the first and only husband and wife singing team in the history of the "Lawrence Welk Show." They didn't start out that way. Ralna auditioned for Lawrence, with Guy accompanying her on the guitar, and *she* was hired! About six months later, Ralna convinced Lawrence to listen to her and Guy sing a duet, and he liked them so much he made them a featured part of every show. Their Southern charm and obvious love for each other make them a natural hit.

When Barbara Boylen "retired," Cissy King was waiting in the wings. She'd been dancing since she was a tot — tap, ballet, ballroom, jazz, modern, everything — often with her brother John, an old friend of Bobby Burgess, as her dancing partner. When Bobby asked John to recommend someone to be his new partner, naturally he put his sister's name at the top of the list. The rest is history! Whether she's doing a polka with Lawrence, or a complicated piece of choreography with Bobby, Cissy is a pro, through and through.

Gail Farrell, Sandi Jensen, and Mary Lou Metzger make up a beautiful trio of melodic voices and pretty faces that not only delight the audiences, but give great joy to Lawrence himself. Gail tagged Lawrence at the Palladium Ballroom in Hollywood and asked for an audition. He told her to go right ahead and sing, and when she had thoroughly captivated everyone, he invited her to appear as a guest on his show. When Tanya Welk left to have her baby, Gail gave up her beauty contest duties as Miss Tulsa, and joined the team permanently. She married lawyer Rick Mallory in 1973, with the entire Welk crew as very special and honored guests.

Sandi Jensen was almost the one to break up the team of Sandi and Salli when she married her college beau, Brent Griffiths, in 1969. But it was Salli who left, and the pretty little blonde stayed on as a very popular solo. The girls were the first of Lawrence's new wave of young performers who called their boss by his first name rather than "Mr." and added a light, modern touch to the show.

A sense of humor and a willingness to work hard made Mary Lou the perfect candidate for Lawrence's brand new "Youth Opportunity Plan." She was just eighteen when Lawrence hired her as an apprentice, and he spent hours helping her go from a talented amateur to a stunning professional. Part of her "training," although not in Lawrence's plans, was finding the man of her dreams, Richard Maloof, a bass and guitar player with the band since 1967. They were married in 1973, and Lawrence beamed with pride that their romance had begun under his own roof. It was a total change in outlook for Lawrence, who used to try and discourage his performers from getting involved with each other. He has, to some extent, moved with the times.

Another of Lawrence's successful and very popular trainees is Anacani, the first Mexican singer on the show. She and her family came to Lawrence's restaurant at Escondido and asked for an audition. She sang him a song in Spanish, and before long, was a singing hostess at the restaurant as part of

her apprenticeship. She shared her greeting duties with another trainee, handsome blond Tom Netherton, whose deep voice, and stunning good looks make him so popular with the ladies.

Family members gather for the annual Christmas show.

The most current members of Lawrence's training program are also the youngest and the most numerous. Lawrence discovered the Semonski Sisters in 1974, and they were a perfect chance to try out his theories on the development of young people. The five sisters, Donna, Joann, Valerie, Audrey, and Michelle had no professional experience when he first heard them sing, and he had the whole family moved into a home in the mobile park at Escondido so he could supervise their training. The two oldest girls, Donna and Joann, worked as cashiers and singing waitresses in his restaurant there, and all five of them had music and harmony lessons, as well as their regular school studies. They worked closely with the people on the show, and four years later, the results are quite obvi-

(Memory Shop)

ous. They are the new Lennons: delightful, adorable, and talented young ladies who have won the hearts of America.

Of course, the Lawrence Welk musical family numbers about fifty, give or take a few, with many faces you recognize from the very first years on TV. Curt Ramsey, Russ Klein, Johnny Szell, Doug Smart, Paul Humphry, the pillars of the orchestra, have been with Lawrence for many years, as has dashing musical director, George Cates. The only female member of the orchestra is Charlotte Harris, a love of a lady

who prefers to keep out of the spotlight, and just be one of the "family."

The "Lawrence Welk Show" and its beloved musical family is a skilled group of performers whose individual talents have been welded together by Lawrence to make the sounds of Champagne Music a continuous and pleasure-giving experience.

Thank you, Lawrence Welk, for sharing your music, and your musical family, with the world.

Production numbers on the "Lawrence Welk Show" are actually quite simple. The maestro prefers to let his stars' talents do all the work.

Meet Lawrence's Musical Family

Lawrence Welk's musical family is a unique and special group of singers, dancers, and musicians. They are talented, personable, and above all, fiercely loyal to Lawrence and everything he stands for. Many of them have appeared in these pages before; some you will be meeting here for the first time. But since his musical family is so very important to Lawrence — and to you — they deserve to stand out on their own.

So, let's get to know the current members of the family. Some of them have been with Lawrence for as long as thirty years, some are newcomers who have just completed their first season with the maestro — the first, we hope, of many.

The Ladies

Norma Zimmer
(The Champagne Lady)
Anacani
Ava Barber
Gail Farrell

Mary Lou Metzger
Sandi Griffiths
Kathie Sullivan
Sheila and Sherry Aldridge

The Gentlemen

Ken Delo
Arthur Duncan
Joe Feeney
Tom Netherton
Bob Ralston
Jim Roberts
Myron Floren
David and Roger Otwell

The Twosomes

Bobby Burgess and Cissy King
Guy and Ralna Hovis

The Band

Henry Cuesta — clarinet, sax
Dick Dale — sax
Bob Davis — sax, clarinet
Dave Edwards — sax
Bob Havens — trombone
Laroon Holt — trumpet
Larry Hooper — piano
Harry Hyams — viola
Jack Imel — drums, marimba, xylophone
John Klein — drums
Russ Klein — sax
Barney Liddell — trombone
Bob Lido — violin
Joe Livotti — concert master
Richard Maloof — trumpet
Mickey McMahon — trumpet
Buddy Merrill — guitar
Charley Parlato — trumpet
Bob Smale — piano
John Zall — trumpet
George Cates — musical supervisor, arranger

Jo Ann Castle spent ten wonderful years playing her ragtime piano and singing with the Welk family. She left to try her luck in nightclubs, with Lawrence as her biggest supporter.

Naturally, we can't tell you everything about everybody, but we will introduce you to the faces and talents featured most frequently in the show. Let's start with the ladies. They are a group of the prettiest, sweetest, most friendly women to ever grace a TV screen, and they all contribute their own very special talents and personalities to the Lawrence Welk musical family.

Norma Zimmer

She is the ultimate Champagne Lady, celebrating eighteen glorious years of wearing that title with grace, charm, and contagious enthusiasm. Lawrence has always said, "If there's perfection in humanity, Norma has it!" Lawrence knows what he's talking about — he's the ultimate perfectionist among bandleaders!

Norma didn't have an easy time growing up. Her family was poor and had to struggle to survive; first in Larson, Idaho, where she was born, and then in Seattle, where they moved when Norma was just five. Her dad was a violin teacher who wanted his daughter to learn the instrument early in life, but voice lessons soon became more important to her. In high school, Norma sang with the school operetta group and in the church choir. She could have gone on to Seattle University, on a music scholarship, had she not decided to try and make it as a professional singer.

It didn't take long for Norma to make her name known in Hollywood. Her beautiful lyric soprano was featured by several of the top choral groups in the country, and she even sang for Lawrence on a number of his record albums.

When Lawrence found himself without a special production number for his 1960 Thanksgiving show, he asked Norma to sing a solo for him. The rest is history. The mail was overwhelming. "More Norma Zimmer," every card and letter demanded, and Lawrence asked her back for New Year's Eve. So charmed was he that Lawrence asked Norma right on the air to join the family, and they've been making beautiful music together ever since.

As dedicated as Norma is to her music and her place on "The Lawrence Welk Show," her own family always comes first. She is married to Randy Zimmer, and they have two fine sons, Ron and Mark. Ron and his wife, Candi, recently made Norma a grandmother for the first time, presenting her with a darling little granddaughter named Kristen.

When Norma's not playing granny, or recording her religious albums, she likes to do a little gardening and painting. The Zimmers live in a trailer court in La Habra, California, that they built and manage themselves. It's hard to imagine where Norma finds the time to do everything, but because of her intense devotion to ever project she undertakes, none of

Even in sophisticated and elegant dresses and gowns, Norma's smile gives her a very special warmth that makes her everybody's favorite.

them every seem to suffer from lack of time.

She is truly a delightful and dedicated lady, and sets an example that everyone follows with pleasure.

Anacani

Anacani (Consuelo) Gil Castillo sang almost as soon as she could talk. That wasn't unusual in her family — everyone was always singing or making music. Her mother, Maria Paula, wanted to be a singer all her life, but her family would not hear of it. Her father, Martin, is a talented guitarist. Anacani's sisters, Flavia, Sylvia, and Anna Maria, play the accordion, violin, and castinets, respectively. Her brothers Vincente and Martin play the guitar and bongoes.

No wonder Anacani was a musical child! Besides her lilting soprano, she is an accomplished pianist and guitarist, and has recently learned to play the accordion, too.

The Castillo family was anxious for their dark-haired little beauty to develop her talents, and when she was ten she started taking professional voice lessons. After graduating from high school, Anacani went with her mother to visit her sister Sylvia in Mexico City. Sylvia was a popular Mexican TV personality, and a producer at one of her rehearsals asked Anacani if she could sing. When she told him she could, and gave an impromptu audition, he immediately booked her on a tour of twenty-five cities and towns in Mexico. It was just the beginning.

The tour ended up near the Castillo family's home town of Escondido, where Lawrence had his popular Country Club Village. Hoping against hope that they might meet him at the Village restaurant, Anacani and her mother went there for dinner. They practically walked right into Lawrence, and Anacani's flashing eyes and beautiful smile made him stop in his tracks. Could she sing? he asked her. She could and did. Lawrence invited her to come back the following night and sing for the patrons at the restaurant. If they liked her as much as he did, he would ask her to appear on his TV show. The diners loved her Spanish songs and beautiful voice, and Anacani made her official debut in January 1973. Within a month she was a regular on the show, as well at a singing hostess as the restaurant.

She is one of Lawrence's most popular ladies. And being

part of the family has taught Anacani so much about life.

"The whole family just sort of adopted me," she says. "And now I have a whole flock of *duennas* to see that I meet the right people, and that I get rid of this complex I didn't even know I had. I wanted to be outgoing, but never could; I was shy and retiring, but I've discovered I love to meet and talk with people of all kinds."

Anacani is still single, and she's in no great hurry to get married. She wants to have children, naturally, and she has even thought of someday being a teacher. Her own family is filled with love and understanding, and she wants to be able to bring that kind of joy to others. That's a quality Lawrence loves about his petite Mexican songstress, and one that her fans adore as well.

If there's anything that has inspired Anacani to become a professional singer, besides her very own musical family, it was, as she says, "the day I first heard Elvis Presley. And then, there were the Beatles. . . ."

Ava Barber

Ava Barber almost didn't make it as a Lawrence Welk regular, but it wasn't her fault. The pretty blonde belle from Knoxville, Tennessee, had sent demo tapes of her songs to Lawrence, and (surprise!) he listened to them and liked them. He suggested that she call him if she ever came to Los Angeles, and he'd try to put her on his show to sing some of her country-and-western songs.

But Ava couldn't afford the plane fare. All was not lost, however, since Lawrence planned to be in Nashville. If she could get there, he'd audition her then.

She got there and sang to Lawrence's accompaniment on the piano. He was enchanted with her rich voice and delightful style, and gave her two plane tickets to California.

With her husband, country-and-western drummer Roger Sullivan, Ava arrived in Los Angeles excited and ready to go. But an industry strike had cancelled production of Lawrence's show, and the end of the dispute was nowhere in sight. There would be no appearance for Ava — at least not then. Disappointed, naturally, but still hopeful, Ava and Roger went home to Knoxville to wait. And just before Christmas their prayers were answered. Lawrence called and

(Ranwood Records)

invited Ava to be on his show in January 1974.

Ava was only nineteen, but music was as much a part of her life as breathing. Her mother, Ruby, led a gospel singing group, and her brother, Gerald, had the top rock-and-roll band in eastern Tennessee. She started singing with Gerald when she was twelve, and has never stopped. When she was fifteen, she cut a record which was a big local success, and for the next four years Ava was a regular on a Knoxville TV show that featured country music. And that's where she met Roger. After a courtship of only five months, just before Ava graduated from high school in 1972, they were married.

It was Roger who set the gears in motion for Ava to meet Lawrence Welk. Her mother suggested she send her tapes to the Welk show, and Roger was in charge of getting them collected and sent to the right address. The only address he could find was for the film laboratory that processed the prints of the TV show, so the tapes took a rather roundabout route before they finally got to Lawrence himself. But he was taken immediately with the strength and power of Ava's voice, and called her as soon as he had heard all her songs.

"It took an awful long time for us to get together," Ava says. "I began to think nothing would ever come of it, but Roger kept telling me that Mr. Welk would come through. Roger had a hunch, and his hunch sure came through beautifully. The strike thing nearly knocked me out. But Roger never wavered. He just kept hoping and working.

"He kept after it like a bulldog, and sure enough, everything happened just like he said it would."

It's been a wonderful four years for Ava, and her popularity with the audience has grown tremendously. She hopes, of course, that it will never end, and indeed her schedule of concert tours and recording dates with the whole Welk family guarantees that Ava will be around for a long time to come.

Charlotte Harris is nicknamed "Charlie" by the rest of the guys in the band. She loves the idea of being just one of the folks, and stays away from publicity and pictures most of the time.

Gail Farrell

One of Lawrence Welk's regular features when he appears at a ballroom is something he calls a "tag dance." Women line up and cut in on Lawrence to have a chance to dance with him. He just loves it; needless to say, so do all the ladies.

On a Saturday night in 1969, one of the ladies who tagged Lawrence for a dance was a smiling, blue-eyed, auburn-haired beauty named Gail Farrell. In the few short minutes they circled the floor, Gail had managed to tell Lawrence that she was a singer with a music degree from Tulsa University in Oklahoma, and had asked him for an audition.

Within an hour or so, she was up there singing in front of a whole ballroom full of people. Lawrence was impressed. He promised he'd be in touch, and he kept his word. He invited Gail to appear on the first show of the new '69–'70 season. And that was just the beginning of a long and solid working relationship.

As far back as she could remember, Gail had always wanted to sing. By the time she was six she already was singing in school concerts and church socials. All through junior high and high school, Gail was part of a singing trio that performed anywhere and everywhere. At Tulsa University, she majored in classical music, hoping someday to teach. One of her roommates was Mary Kay Place, who later went on to become Loretta in the TV series "Mary Hartman, Mary Hartman."

Because Gail was so pretty, she got involved in several beauty contests. She began to realize that she liked being up there in front of people and enjoyed entertaining them. So when the opportunity to "tag" Lawrence came up, Gail saw it as her golden chance.

As part of the Welk family, Gail had another, and rather unexpected opportunity. When the group flew to Waikiki Beach for a special show in 1973, the airlines executive who made all the arrangements — a good friend of Lawrence's — was so taken with Gail that he introduced her to his son, Richard Mallory. A short time later, Gail married him, and the whole Welk crew was there to help them celebrate.

Mary Lou Metzger

Mary Lou is doubly a member of Lawrence's musical family. Not only is she a favorite with everyone on the show, charming them with her delightful bubbly voice and personality, but she is married to another family member, Richard Maloof, a bass and tuba player.

The dark-haired, green-eyed little beauty is a Pennsylvania native; she was born in Pittsburgh and moved to Philadelphia with her family when she was five. Her mother was a pianist and her dad a violinist, so music came quite naturally to Mary

Lou. By the time she got to Temple University, she had decided to major in music and drama, and for two years that's exactly what she did.

Then came a chance too good to pass up: an audition for Arthur Godfrey's "All American College Show." She was an instant success, and three days after the audition was on her way to Los Angeles to rehearse.

A family friend suggested she audition for Lawrence while she was in Hollywood, and so she did. The timing was just perfect. Norma Zimmer was out of town, and Lawrence needed a voice for a recording session. Mary Lou filled in, and Lawrence asked her to guest on his show and also to join the troupe in Lake Tahoe for their annual summer tour. She's been with them ever since.

The pretty ladies on the "Lawrence Welk Show" harmonize voices as well as good looks. Left to right: Sandi Jensen, Ralna Hovis, Mary Lou Metzger and Gail Farrell.

Mary Lou has an impressive list of stage credits, and she came to Lawrence with a varied background in musical comedy and drama. She appeared in the national company of *The Music Man,* and had parts in various productions of *My Fair Lady, Lady In The Dark, Most Happy Fella, Kiss Me Kate, Carousel, The Sound Of Music,* and *The King And I.* She even had a bit role in *Cycad,* a movie starring Gary Merrill and Sammy Davis, Jr.

It's no wonder Mary Lou was able to assure her position on the Welk show when she substituted for Tanya Welk in a big production number. She played a Betty Boop–type character, was absolutely delightful, and easily became a full-fledged member of the family.

Sandi Griffiths

Like so many others in Lawrence Welk's musical family, Sandi Griffiths has been singing since she was a child. She was encouraged by her father, a music lover all his life, and by the time she was five was a regular on Art Linkletter's TV show. On her first appearance, she announced to the audience that she was going to be a singer when she grew up, and so made her official debut right then and there. Now she remembers it was not much of a song and she was not much of a singer, but that she loved the feeling of singing in front of lots of people, and seeing them enjoy what she was doing.

Sandi continued singing all through school; and in college, at Brigham Young University, she teamed up with Salli Flynn. After a summer of singing at Disneyland, the girls decided to drop out of school for a while and become professionals so they could be part of a USO tour sent to entertain the American troops in Vietnam. Their three-week stint convinced them; they decided not to go back to school in order to concentrate on their professional careers.

They were fussy about their bookings and held out for what they felt were the right ones. Soon the opportunity came along to open for Jack Jones in Harrah's at Lake Tahoe. That's where they heard that Lawrence Welk would be holding an open audition in Hollywood later in the summer.

Sandi and Salli were just one act out of the 250 that showed up for that audition, and they were the only performers Lawrence chose. After three guest appearances on the show the audience response was so overwhelming that Lawrence asked them to be regulars. That summer of 1967 was for them the most exciting one ever.

Five years later, Sandi found she was a solo act. Salli left to pursue a separate career, and Sandi was a little worried that Lawrence might not need just another singer.

She needn't have been concerned. Lawrence was so enchanted and enthused by his pretty redhead, that he immediately found new things for her to do. Her job was never really in doubt, and today, as a solo performer or as part of a sparkling trio with Gail Farrell and Mary Lou Metzger, Sandi is firmly entrenched in the family group.

Sandi is starting her own personal family circle, too. She and her husband Brent Griffiths have three delightful children, Jenni, Ami, and baby Benji. She has the best of two worlds: a wonderful home and family, and a terrific career. And she just couldn't be happier.

Kathie Sullivan

The girl with the golden voice had a very tough decision to make when Lawrence Welk offered her a chance to join his entourage. Should she accept, or should she finish up her last nine credits at the University of Wisconsin?

The solution was to do both. She flew to Los Angeles and appeared on the show until the season was over, then she went back to Madison and earned herself a bachelor's degree in voice.

Lynn Anderson was a favorite for many years. She also left the show to try and make it on her own.

She didn't start out as a voice student. Back in high school, Kathie started playing the violin, though not exactly by choice. It was the only instrument in the school orchestra that was available free, and Kathie couldn't afford to rent or buy anything else. So violin it was, until the orchestra teacher loaned her his cello. He also urged her to study voice, so she joined the *a capella* choir, and continued studying classical music throughout college. Her hope was to become an opera singer.

She joined the university's "Swing Choir," and was chosen to participate in a USO tour of Greenland, Iceland, and Labrador. The group changed its name to the "State Street Revue" and appeared in small clubs all over Wisconsin, as well as on a campus TV show.

Then Kathie heard about Lawrence Welk's Champagne Lady contest, a local promotional event that she entered and won hands down. The prize was a guest appearance with Lawrence at his Madison concert date, and he was so enthusiastic about her voice that he offered her a job. That's when she had her big decision to make.

Kathie has switched her allegiance from opera to gospel music. She's always been a churchgoer and, like Lawrence, finds church music inspirational and fulfilling. She's signed up with the same agent Norma Zimmer uses and has been spending her free time doing gospel concerts and crusade performances. If anything solidifies Lawrence's trust and confidence in one of his performers, it's a strong religious conviction. Kathie certainly fills the bill.

Sherry and Sheila Aldridge

Persistence pays off; at least it does with Lawrence Welk!

Sherry and Sheila Aldridge had been Lawrence Welk fans for as long as they could remember. They had watched his TV show every week with their parents, Talton and Jacqueline, and hoped that some day they would even be able to appear on it themselves.

Their father, Talton Aldridge, had been a composer, singer, and musician in the thirties and fourties and the Aldridge house was always filled with music. The girls were members of the Baptist church choir, and sang in school and community concerts.

Sherry took voice lessons, and Sheila was very active in the musical community at home. They were both regulars on WPTX Radio in Lexington Park, Maryland and were always singing, either together or alone. After high school, they went to Miami to visit their older sister Sue and liked it so much they decided to stay for a while. Sherry became a stewardess and Sheila went into sales before deciding to try stewardessing herself. After a year, both girls felt they had had enough of the high-flying life and went home to Knoxville to start singing again. They decided, too, that they would find out everything they could about Lawrence Welk, and make it their business to meet him as soon as possible.

By sheer bravado, they managed to audition for him one night in Nashville. He was charmed, but there just wasn't any room on the show for any more singers. He did tell them to call him if they ever came to Los Angeles.

That was all the girls needed to hear. They finished up their club date in Knoxville and got on a plane for Los Angeles faster than you could say Sheila and Sherry Aldridge.

They arrived at Lawrence's office and persuaded the receptionist to at least let them say hello to Lawrence. He remembered them, of course, but again, impressed as he was with their singing, told them there just weren't any openings on the show.

The sisters were not about to accept defeat. They came back the next morning to talk with Lawrence once more. He happened to be speaking with his manager on the phone, and arranged for the girls to meet with him the next morning. Taping for the new season wouldn't begin for six weeks, but Lawrence and his manager promised they'd try to work something out.

There was hope. Sherry and Sheila went home to Knoxville, and for those next six weeks were on pins and needles. When the waiting was over, they flew back to Los Angeles and once again arrived at Lawrence's office to see him.

It was their lucky day. Lawrence was with his lawyer, and they were both tremendously impressed with Sherry's and Sheila's version of the Everly Brothers' song "All I Have to Do Is Dream." Lawrence took them to see the show's producer-director, who was as enthusiastic as Lawrence himself. They were introduced on the premiere show of the '78 TV season. An instant smash, they are now counted among the regulars, both on the show, and as singing hostesses at Escondido.

After so many rejections, the sisters' perseverance finally did pay off — they reminded Lawrence of himself, and he had to give them a fair chance.

When Andra Willis left Lawrence in 1969, it was to be able to spend more time with her husband. She gave the maestro plenty of advance notice, and their parting was a pleasant one.

The Twosomes
Bobby and Cissy

If ever two people were made for each other, Bobby and Cissy are the ones. They dance in such perfect harmony, it's hard to believe they haven't been dancing together since the time they were just starting to walk.

Actually, Cissy King is Bobby Burgess's second partner. The

first, Barbara Boylen, left the show when she got married, and Bobby was stranded without a complementary pair of feet. He remembered an old dancing competitor, John King, and asked him to recommend someone. John suggested his kid sister, Cissy, and the meeting was a magic one. She and Bobby hit it off from the first foxtrot and there's never been any doubt; they were simply destined to dance together.

Cissy's been dancing up a storm since she was three years old. By the time Bobby was thirteen, and about to become a Mouseketeer, he had already been on more than sixty TV shows — dancing all the way.

Bobby met his first dancing partner, Barbara Boylen, when he was still in high school and they won ballroom competitions all over the country. They took Lawrence's Calcutta Dance Contest with a special routine that Bobby choreographed, and he just kept coming up with newer and better dance numbers every time Lawrence turned around.

When Bobby's not at home in the Hollywood Hills with his beautiful wife, Kristie, who's Myron Floren's daughter, and their baby girl, Becki Jane; or rehearsing with Cissy to perfect one of the 200 routines in their varied and always exciting repertoire; you can probably find him in front of a bunch of eager and, hopefully, fleet-footed dance students. Bobby teaches dance for TV and film at the University of Southern California, and that's almost as big a thrill for him as creating new and different dance routines to keep his and Cissy's television fans spellbound.

(Memory Shop)

Guy and Ralna are the first and only husband-and-wife singing team on Lawrence's show. But they were irresistible to Lawrence, and certainly to the millions who watch them each week.

Right: Bobby Burgess and Cissy King have been dancing together for many years. They do anything from a little soft shoe to ballroom-style dancing: tap, modern, even a little apache now and then. They are an extremely talented pair.

Ralna and Guy

Ralna English started singing when she was "tiny," and just never stopped. Guy Hovis planned to be an accountant until he won a talent contest while he was in the army.

Fortunately, from entirely different routes, both Ralna and Guy wound up at "The Horn," a Santa Monica club where young hopefuls performed, waiting to be "discovered." Ralna thought Guy was just a kid, and it wasn't until he convinced her that he was really two years older than she that they started to date. Their romance flourished between appearances at The Horn, and they were married in 1969.

They never even considered singing together. Ralna had arrived in Los Angeles via school and local TV appearances in

(Memory Shop)

Bobby and Cissy display their versatility in a Roaring Twenties number.

her native Texas, and the world of TV commercials in Dallas. She had been on the road with Frank Sinatra, Jr. and the Kirby Stone Four, and on an eight-week USO tour of Korea, Japan, and Thailand.

But all those nights at the club were preparing Ralna for one thing: her great ambition to appear on "The Lawrence Welk Show." None of her family had ever seen her appear anywhere, but since they all loved Lawrence, it was the natural place for Ralna to make her debut. A Welk talent scout saw her at The Horn, but nothing happened through him. She and Guy went to see Lawrence personally, and once he heard Ralna himself, there was never any question. She made only three guest appearances before Lawrence asked her to become a regular.

Guy had no great ambition to be a Welk personality. He was happy appearing at The Horn and on various TV shows. If Ralna hadn't insisted that Lawrence listen to the two of them do a special number they had prepared just for him, Ralna and Guy might never have become the first (and only) married couple in the history of the Welk show to perform together regularly. They are so popular that they get almost as much fan mail as Lawrence himself. And it's easy to see why. They are loving and lovely on stage, and it's all very much for real.

The Gentlemen
Ken Delo

Ken Delo is a man of many talents. His repertoire reads like a one-man variety show: he sings, dances, acts, does monologues, and performs magic tricks. All of which make him a perfect member of the multitalented Lawrence Welk family.

When Ken was just eleven, he decided to step into the shoes of the great magician, Blackstone, and bought himself a book about magic. Armed with that and his natural performing bent, he delighted his schoolmates with his feats of prestidigitation. If that weren't enough, he also mimed the most popular records of the day, and formed a quartet to sing at school dances and shows.

He was so good, and so very entertaining, that WXYZ in Detroit made him a regular on one of their TV variety shows. He stayed with them until he joined the army and started putting his talents to use with the "Fifth Army Casuals," a bunch of GIs who performed on radio, TV, and stage for the Public Information Office of the army's Fifth Headquarters in Chicago. It was fun, it was rewarding, and it was Ken's first real step toward a professional career.

The next logical place for him to try out his talents was Los Angeles, and he promptly landed a part in a *Gay Nineties* show at the Hollywood Bowl. His ambition to succeed took him all over southern California on a whistle-stop tour of one-nighters; and up to Alaska where he played for seven weeks to members of the armed forces.

From the bitter cold of Alaska, Ken then went to the other temperature extreme — to Australia, for an eight-week tour of nightclubs and TV shows. He wound up staying for six months, and made over eighty appearances on TV there. He even produced, wrote, and starred in his own weekly TV show, and won Australian television's highest honor — the award for "Best National Variety Show." Strictly by chance, he met a dancer named Arthur Duncan in Australia, and four years after that fateful meeting, in May 1969, Arthur introduced Ken to Lawrence Welk. Ken was a natural. Lawrence put him on the show right away, and within weeks he was the newest face in Lawrence's ever-increasing bunch of regulars.

Ken is a family man, married to Marilyn Makhart, a former

ballerina, and the father of Kimberly, eight, and Kevin, five. But that doesn't stop him from being a favorite with the ladies, especially when he heads down into the audience and sings directly to the "special girl" he has chosen for the song. When Ken bats his baby brown eyes, there's no doubt that he's a charmer through and through. Those precious moments on the show become distinctly his own.

(Memory Shop)

Arthur Duncan executes one of his fancy flying steps for the audience. He's been with Lawrence for many years, and can't imagine what he'd do if he ever had to stop dancing.

Arthur Duncan

Arthur Duncan is one of those rare birds, a native Californian. He was born in Pasadena, and never intended to get into show business; all he wanted was some money to work his way through college.

As a kid, he used to sing along with jukebox records, and occasionally an appreciative listener would toss him a quarter or so. And in junior high school, he was more or less drafted into being part of a dancing quartet for school performances. Even at Pasadena City College he sang and danced mostly for the money and the pure enjoyment of it all — until it became so lucrative that he decided to leave school and try show business for real.

He was successful beyond his wildest dreams, making lots of appearances on nationally televised variety shows, and appearing with top-name entertainers in nightclubs. Ten days with Jimmy Rodgers in Australia turned into five years of touring Europe and the East, and his own weekly TV show "down under." His wife Donna, whom he had met in San Jose in 1953 and married a year later, was with him all the time. And she became almost as immersed in the world of show business as Arthur.

The Duncans returned to the States in 1964, and Arthur was immediately booked into Los Angeles's Basin Street West with Lionel Hampton. It was there that Lawrence's personal manager saw him and arranged for Arthur to make a guest appearance on the show. The first one led to five more, and Arthur was a Welk regular. He and Donna love the traveling that the show tour entails, and since Arthur is the eighth child in a huge family of thirteen, there are plenty of brothers and sisters and nieces and nephews all over the country to visit and spend time with during those traveling months.

The terrific threesome is made up of the dancing feet of Jack Imel, Arthur Duncan and Bobby Burgess.

Joe Feeney

His lilting Irish tenor is always a treat; it's a voice Lawrence Welk fans look forward to eagerly each week. And for Joe, that's the greatest praise of all.

From the time he was just a wee lad with a soprano voice in the church choir in Grand Island, Nebraska, he always knew that music would be his life. Just out of high school, he won a guest shot on Horace Heidt's "Youth Opportunity Hour," and headed into the army, confident that there was opportunity for music there, too. And he was right. He won several singing contests, and a spot on Arlene Francis's "Talent Patrol" TV show.

When he got out of the army, he went to the University of Nebraska. It held special memories for him since during his freshman year he met Georgia LeGryva. She had heard his beautiful voice one day through an open window, and fell head over heels in love with the man who owned it. They were married shortly after.

Joe never did get to finish school. By the time their second child arrived (they now have ten), Joe had taken a job as a salesman and had pretty much given up music and school. But luck was with him. A friend sent a tape of his singing to

Lawrence who was looking for new voices for a special TV show, "Top Tunes and New Talent." Lawrence was totally delighted with Joe's beautiful voice. So in 1956, Joe joined the Welk family, and he's been one of their most regular regulars ever since.

Joe Feeney and Mary Lou Metzger make beautiful music together. Their duets are a highlight, and they both seem to enjoy them as much as the audience does.

Myron Floren

Who doesn't know Myron Floren? Of all the Welk personalities, he is probably the best known. Myron is — next to Lawrence himself — the performer most in demand for personal appearances. His good-natured sense of humor and his nimble-fingered accordion playing make him number one on the public's most-wanted list. He manages to clock in an astonishing two-hundred thousand extra miles of touring every year, besides appearing weekly with Lawrence and adding his own invaluable talents to the administration of the band itself.

The story of the Welk-Floren association is a well-known one. Everybody thought Lawrence was absolutely crazy to hire another — and better — accordionist. But Lawrence insisted. He knew just how good Myron was, and just how much that extraordinary talent would add to the band. That was twenty-eight years ago, and since then Lawrence has proven right a million times over.

Myron loves to play polkas, which perhaps endears him to Lawrence more than anything else, but he's also adept at everything from Broadway show tunes to classical compositions. He's written several songs himself, and has recorded several albums on his own. He has also written a series of instruction books on how to play the accordion; something he is eminently fitted to do.

One of Myron's proudest moments on the Welk show came when his oldest daughter, Kristie (there are five girls altogether), married dancer Bobby Burgess. It was a gala affair, and a romantic one, too. They were married on Valentine's Day, and Myron had tears of happiness in his eyes throughout the entire ceremony.

Tom Netherton

Blond, blue-eyed, and six foot, five inches tall, Tom Netherton is a genuine dreamboat. His handsome face and rich baritone make him a natural favorite with the ladies, and through it all, he's managed to stay single!

Tom was an army child, born in Munich, Germany, and living in Georgia, North Carolina, Kansas, and Chicago before the family settled down in Bloomington, a suburb of Minneapolis.

He was never interested in a show-business career. In the fourth grade he sang in a Christmas pageant, and in junior high won the lead in the school musical — on a dare from his best friend. But that was about it. He was more interested in track sports and in climbing the Andes mountains as part of his senior year as an exchange student in Peru.

When he entered the University of Minnesota, he decided to study architecture, but he had difficulty keeping his grades high enough to keep him out of the draft. So he dropped out of school and went into the Officers Candidate School of the army. He was a second lieutenant in Panama when he started singing at the officer's club, and he was hooked. He became entertainment officer, and found himself truly enjoying what he was doing.

During all this, Tom felt as if something was missing in his life, and he discovered that it was a real relationship with God. He started attending meetings of a Christian group, and at twenty-one, started his life all over again. Then "at twenty-four," he says, "I gave my life to Christ, a decision which changed the direction of my whole life, and afforded me a truly solid foundation in terms of having an actual personal relationship with Him."

Tom went on to study the Bible, but felt torn between his desire to devote his life to religious study and practice, and his need to still be part of the entertainment world. It was the example of Pat Boone, who found the way to do both, that helped Tom make his decision.

While Tom was appearing with a show in North Dakota, he was introduced to Lawrence Welk. He sang three songs for him, and Lawrence asked him to appear with the group in St. Paul. Tom did so, and was absolutely flabbergasted when Lawrence asked him to make a guest appearance on his TV program. Tom packed up and went to Los Angeles in a flash. He made his debut on the 1972 Christmas show, and he's been with Lawrence ever since.

His good looks, beautiful voice, and honesty and sincerity

Myron Floren is Lawrence's right-hand man, a protégé, so to speak. No one, least of all Lawrence, minds that Myron is, without a doubt, the best accordionist on the show. That's what made Lawrence hire him in the first place!

are inspirations to everyone, and his strong belief in making music work as an uplifting force for people all over the world has given him a very special place in the Welk family.

David and Roger Otwell

You could never hope to find more decidedly identical twins than these twenty-two-year-old brothers from the Texas farm lands. They can even take turns to be the older one, since there was some mix-up at the hospital, and no one really knows for sure who was born first. But it hardly matters; twins are a family trait. Their father is one, and their mother has twin cousins. David and Roger have two older siblings, brother Von Dean, an electrical engineer, and a sister, Barbara Love.

The boys got into music by playing the tuba in their high school marching band and singing in their church choir. They won music scholarships to Lubbock Christian College, where they wrote music and sang together in the choir, and were members of "The Good Time Singers."

They moved on to West Texas State University to study harmonics, but after they took a summer off to earn money for the upcoming year's tuition, found that their jobs at a music store, whch allowed them to sing at any town event that came up, were much more fun and rewarding than school. So they never went back, but instead started entertaining at every possible function in town — weddings, dances, proms, you name it, the Otwells sang at it.

They decided to send Lawrence Welk some tapes of their singing. It was a lucky shot. Lawrence called and asked them to come to Los Angeles to appear on his TV show. The boys were greeted with such warmth and enthusiasm by Lawrence that they were bent immediately on becoming permanent members of the show.

And so they have. Don't forget, Lawrence was an ex-farm boy himself, so there's a natural alliance between him and these two young brothers who are so totally dedicated to their music they can't help but remind him of his own youth down on the farm in Strasburg. And there's nothing Lawrence likes better than helping talented youngsters make it in the music world.

Barbara Boylen with Bobby Burgess.

Bob Ralston

Lawrence Welk discovered Bob when he was just fifteen, the winner of a brand new car in a local "Hollywood Opportunity" TV special. Lawrence didn't take Bob on the show then; Bob was too young and too busy doing many other things.

Not only was he studying the piano and accompanying dance students, but he had been playing with the Salvation Army Band and raising hamsters in the family garage for a neat little profit. He was getting so wrapped up in his music, though, that the budding entrepreneur gave up the hamster business and simply wrote a book on how to raise and care for them.

By the time he got to high school, Bob was into photography and the garage turned into a darkroom; another profitable business venture for this ambitious young man.

All the while, he was still studying music. He had advanced from the piano to the baritone horn and the trombone. In 1964, he graduated from the University of Southern California with a degree in composition and accompaniment.

Lawrence "found" him again when one of his arrangers recommended Bob for a recording date. He had been playing with Freddy Martin at Los Angeles's Coconut Grove, proving himself equally adept at a variety of instruments, including piano, organ, and bells.

His range of talents was so impressive that Lawrence couldn't help but invite him on the show for a guest appearance in the spring of 1962. Bob just kept on being invited back, almost every week until June 1963, when Lawrence surprised him right on stage and asked him to be a show regular.

It's been a happy fifteen years for Bob, and for Lawrence, of course. Lawrence shines with pride whenever the whole Ralston family — Bob, his Dutch-born wife, Fietje, and their two children, Randy and Dianne — make a holiday appearance with the rest of the Welk family.

(Memory Shop)

Joe Feeney is the leader of this band of natty musicians. He puts his Irish tenor to good use every week.

Jim Roberts

Another "old-timer" with Lawrence and the family, Jim has been with the group since 1954. He cornered Lawrence at the old Aragon Ballroom where the Champagne Music Makers

(Memory Shop)

Barbara Boylen was Bobby Burgess's original dancing partner, from college days on. She left the show to get married, but everyone remembers her sparkling smile and her extraordinary talent.

had a steady gig, and charmed his way into the hearts of everyone. He was right there when the "Lawrence Welk Show" debuted on national TV in 1955.

Jim always sang as a child, in school glee clubs and church choirs, and later on in the army with his fellow GI's. He started doing musical comedy seriously when he got out of the service, and built himself a respectable career with the Los Angeles Civic Light Opera Association, singing the lead in such musical favorites as *Girl Crazy, Desert Song, Rio Rita, Finnian's Rainbow,* and *Song of Norway.*

In between all these singing engagements, Jim married Jane Silk, a former Earl Carroll beauty, and they have two handsome sons, Steven and Gary. They live just a stone's throw away from the studio, so Jim is always on time for work. Not that he'd ever be late in any case. He's a dedicated member of the family — and one of its most popular ones.

The Band
Henry Cuesta

Music was a way of life for Henry from his earliest beginnings. His father, Miguel, was a classical violinist and teacher who started his son on the road to learning music when he was still a small boy. And Henry's cousin — his idol, in fact — was Ernie Caceras, Glenn Miller's top baritone saxophone and clarinet player. It was a thrill to hear cousin Ernie play, and Henry couldn't wait until he could learn the sax and the clarinet himself.

And learn he did! Along with the instruments themselves, he discovered jazz, Benny Goodman, and the art of improvisation. It all payed off while he was in the army, stationed in Stuttgart, Germany. The Stuttgart Symphony Orchestra found itself without a clarinetist to play that all important opening section of Gershwin's *Rhapsody in Blue*. The orchestra called the army for reinforcements, and they sent Henry.

He was the perfect choice. His experience served him well when he got out of the army and appeared with the Toronto Symphony Orchestra in their "Jazz Night at the Symphony" and Toronto became his new home town. Besides the city's receptiveness to the jazz sounds that Henry loved so much, his new bride, Janette McFater, was a Toronto native. What better reason to stay in one place!

Another jazz great, Bobby Hackett, heard Henry at Toronto's Skyline Hotel and suggested he get in touch with George Thow about a solo spot that was open in the Lawrence Welk band.

It was an inviting idea, and Henry followed it up right away. He sent along some of his recordings; they were forwarded to Lawrence, and he was hired by phone.

In the six years he's been with Lawrence, Henry has won the hearts of jazz fans all over the country. His evenings with Lawrence and some of the finest symphony orchestras in the country — Salt Lake City, Denver, Nashville, to name just a few — have been exceptionally fine entertainment, and joyous occasions for Henry. If you ask him what the greatest moments in his career have been, Henry will tell you they were his five years with Jack Teagarden's orchestra, the Stuttgart Symphony appearance, his years in Toronto, and above all, his happy times with the Lawrence Welk Show.

Dick Dale

He sings, he acts, he plays a mean saxophone, and in his twenty-seven years with the Lawrence Welk family, Dick Dale has become one of the best-loved performers on the show.

He first met up with Lawrence in Iowa, Dick's home state, He played and sang for Lawrence, but there was just no opening in the band at the time. Three months later, when Lawrence was playing at the Trianon Ballroom in Chicago, the opportunity came.

Dick had been playing with dance bands since he graduated from high school in 1942 — with time out to join the navy in 1944. When he came home from the service in 1946, he took up his career again, and became a member of a popular Midwest orchestra, "The Six Fat Dutchmen." They were five after Lawrence's call to Dick in 1951, when Dick happily went to California with the Welk band and was there when Lawrence and company made their television debut.

Larry Hooper

Larry's a true Welk veteran, having joined up with Lawrence in 1948, adding his virtuoso piano playing and deep baritone to the Music Makers while they were appearing at New York's Roosevelt Hotel.

Music was always his first priority, even though as a kid he had to juggle his piano practice with his baseball games. But he persevered, and finally joined the staff band of KWKH Radio in Shreveport, Louisiana right after high school graduation. He went on to play with several big bands in the early forties, and when Lawrence's offer came along, it was one he couldn't refuse.

Neil Levang

Neil started off as a one-week guest substitute on the "Lawrence Welk Show" in 1959 when guitarist Buddy Merrill went into the army. After a first performance, the one-week engagement turned into one lasting almost twenty years.

Here was another musician with a background remarkably similar to Lawrence's own. Neil is also the son of a farmer, from Adams, North Dakota, and his first instrument — a banjo, not an accordion — was also a family heirloom. By the time Neil was fifteen, he had traveled all over the country with various bands, and had been an early morning D.J. for a Seattle radio station. He spent some years in the Coast Guard, and then came to Los Angeles to pick up his musical career. He played with groups like the Modernaires and the Four Preps, as well as recording with many of the large film companies. When he came to Lawrence, his reputation as one of the finest guitarists in the business had preceded him right through the door.

Bob Lido

For twenty-four years, Bob has been surprising audiences with his remarkable range and expertise on the violin. He's been playing since he was a child in Jersey City, New Jersey, and he was so diligent about his music that he later became a featured performer with Carmen Cavalaro's band, and Perry Como's Supper Club. When he joined Lawrence in 1952, he quickly proved that he was as equally at home with tender ballads as he was with country music and jazz favorites, and so was the natural choice for leader when Lawrence decided to revive his Hotsy Totsy Band to add a little nostalgia and an occasional touch of humor to the show.

Jack Imel

If ever there was a prototype for jack-of-all-trades, Mr. Imel is it. He does everything, and does everything well — from a better-than-average soft shoe, to an unequaled expertise on the marimba.

Jack was another new young star whom Lawrence featured on his "Top Tunes and New Talent" shows in the late fifties. Jack was straight out of the United States Navy where he had won the all-navy talent contest and appeared on Ed Sullivan's all-navy TV show. He was so good that Ed asked him back again the next year, and Lawrence offered him a full-time job just as soon as his navy discharge was final.

He's become absolutely irreplaceable to Lawrence, not just as a fine performer — in whatever capacity he's working — but as the man in charge of the road shows. He has terrific ability for details, and Lawrence can be sure nothing will go

(Frank Edwards Fotos International)

The Semonski Sisters are Lawrence's latest protégés. They will probably be as popular with Welk fans as the Lennons were years ago.

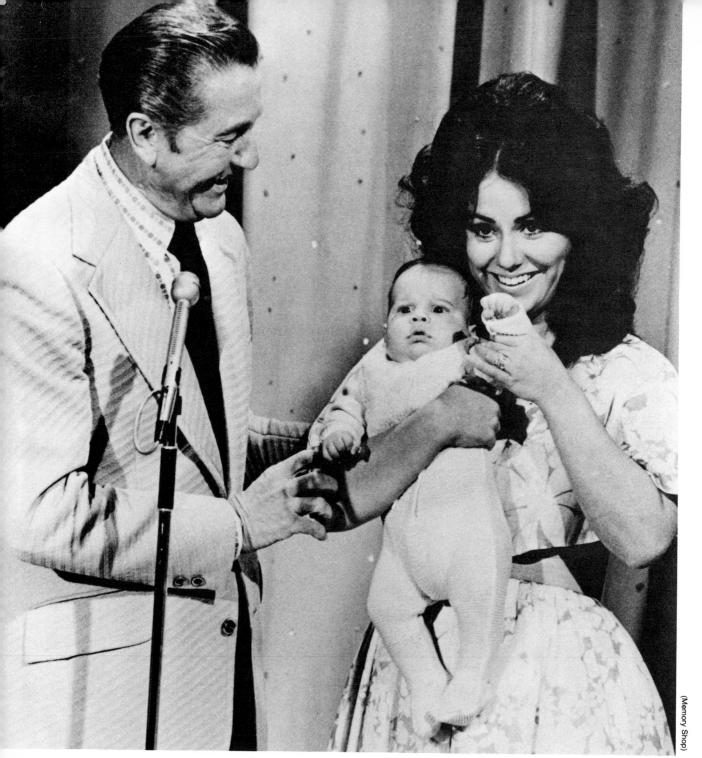

(Memory Shop)

Lawrence's proudest moment came when his daughter-in-law, Tanya Falan Welk, presented him with a grandson named Lawrence Welk III.

wrong as long as Jack's in command.

Hope you've enjoyed getting to know some of the wonderful people who make "The Lawrence Welk Show" a weekly delight. Whether they've worked for Lawrence for one year or thirty, they all share his zest for performing and keeping the audience happy. The dedicated members of Lawrence Welk's musical family are truly a close-knit group, both onstage and off.

Recordings by Lawrence Welk

ALBUMS

Best of Lawrence Welk	MCA 2-4044
Best of Lawrence Welk #2	MCA 2-4046
Best of Lawrence Welk's Polkas	MCA 2-4104
Best of Lawrence Welk	RAN 8162*
Big Band's Greatest Hits	COL CG30009
Calcutta	RAN 8024
Candida	RAN 8083
Champagne Music of Lawrence Welk	RAN 8023
Champagne Music of Lawrence Welk	COR 20100
Champagne Polkas	VOC 73865
Country Music's Greatest Hits	RAN 8027
Favorites from the Golden 60s	RAN 8068
Galveston	RAN 8049
Go Away Little Girl	RAN 8091
Best of Golden Hits	RAN 8028
Hymns We Love	RAN 8042
I Love You Truly	RAN 8053
In Concert	RAN 6001
Love Is Blue	RAN 8003
Memories	RAN 8044
Moon River	RAN 8016
Nadia's Theme	RAN 8165*
Polka and Waltz Time	COR 20053
Polkas	RAN 8014
Polkas and Other Favorites	SPB 4052
Polkas on Parade	TRD 2111
Reminiscing	RAN 5001
Silent Night	RAN 8020
Songs of the Islands	RAN 8022
That's Entertainment	RAN 8130
Till the End of Time	VOC 73888
To America with Love	RAN 8030
22 Great Waltzes	RAN 7004*
200 Years of American Music	RAN 7002*
Waltz Time	RAN 8025

* = most current releases

Lawrence Welk's Big Band Sound	RAN 8077
Lawrence Welk Celebrates 50 Years in Music	RAN 6002
Lawrence Welk Celebrates 25 Years on TV	RAN 8145
Lawrence Welk's Champagne Strings	RAN 9079
Lawrence Welk's Most Requested TV Favorites	RAN 8140
Lawrence Welk's Singers	RAN 8034
Lawrence Welk's TV Show	RAN 8026
Lawrence Welk Presents:	
His Favorite German Orchestra and Singers	RAN 8101
The Clarinet of Henry Cuesta	RAN 8166
Dick Kessner	BRU 754044
Bob Ralston	RAN 8031
Myron Floren's New Sounds	RAN 8005
Winchester Cathedral	RAN 8017
Wonderful Music of Lawrence Welk	VOC 73921
Yellow Bird	RAN 8021

SINGLES

Baretta's Theme/Paloma Blanca	RAN 1073*
Beer Barrel Polka/Pennsylvania Polka	MCA 60081
Nadia's Theme/Johnny's Theme	RAN 1068

Abbreviations:

RAN	Ranwood Records	VOC	Vocalion Records (MCA)
GRT	GRT Records	BRU	Brunswick Records
COR	Coral Records	MCA	MCA Records
SPB	Springboard Records	COL	Columbia Records

Two of Lawrence Welk's most popular stars, Myron Floren and Champagne Lady Norma Zimmer, have also recorded several albums. Myron has a total of eighteen, his most current being:

Nashville Sessions	GRT 8019
22 Great Polkas	RAN 7005

Norma Zimmer has recorded five albums with Welk star, Jim Roberts, all inspirational, on WORD Records. Her latest solo album is:

Norma	RAN 8169

Index

Aldridge, Sheila and Sherry, 82, 92–93
Anacani, 78, 79, 82, 85–86
Anderson, Lynn, 72

Barber, Ava, 82, 86–87
Bernhardi, Lee, 69
Best, Lois, 53
Blenders, The, 72
Bobby and Cissy, 94
Boylen, Barbara, 72, 76, 77
Buckeyes, The, 76
Burgess, Bobby, 72, 76, 77, 78, 83, 94

Castle, Jo Ann, 73
Cates, George, 80, 83
Cathcart, Dick, 69
Champagne Ladies, 51–62
Clark, Mahlon, 99
Cromer, Bob, 54
Cuesta, Henry, 83, 105

Dale, Dick, 83, 106
Davis, Bob, 83
Delo, Ken, 77, 83, 97, 98
Dixon, Greg, 72
Duncan, Arthur, 76–77, 83, 98
Duncan, Donna, 77
Durante, Jimmy, 68

Edwards, Dave, 83
English, Ralna (Mrs. Guy Hovis) 77, 83, 94, 96

Falan, Tanya (Mrs. Lawrence Welk, Jr.), 62, 68, 70, 78
Farrell, Gail, 78, 82, 87–88
Fedderson, Don, 34, 40
Feeney, Joe, 77, 83, 99–100
Floren, Kristie, 76
Floren, Myron, 74, 76, 83, 100
Flynn, Salli, 73, 78
Fountain, Pete, 72

Gass, Dick, 69
Grey, Maxine, 53
Griffiths, Sandi, 82, 90–91

Harris, Charlotte, 80
Hart, Clay, 74
Havens, Bob, 83

Herman, Jules, 53
Holt, Laroon, 83
Hooper, Larry, 83, 106
Hovis, Guy, 77, 80, 94, 96
Humphry, Paul, 80
Hyams, Harry, 83

Imel, Jack, 77, 80, 107–108
Imel, Norma, 77

Jensen, Sandi, 78

Kelly, Alma, 15–16
Kelly, George, 15–17
King, Cissy, 76, 77–78, 83, 94
King, John, 78
Klein, John, 83
Klein, Russ, 80, 83

Lawrence Welk and His Champagne Music Makers, 24
Lawrence Welk and His Honolulu Fruit Gum Orchestra, 22
Lawrence Welk and His Hotsy Totsy Boys, 17
Lennon Sisters, the, 64–69
Levang, Neil 106–107
Liddell, Barney, 83
Lido, Bob, 83, 107
Lincoln Boulds Orchestra, The, 14
Linn, Roberta, 54
Livotti, Joe, 83
Lon, Alice, 55–57

Mallory, Rick, 78
Maloof, Richard, 78, 83
McMahon, Richard, 83
Merrill, Buddy, 83
Metzger, Mary Lou, 78, 82, 88–90
Miller High Life, 26
Mowery, Joan, 53–54

Netherton, Tom, 79, 83, 100–102
Nevins, Natalie, 70, 72

Otwell, David and Roger, 83, 102

Parlato, Buddy, 83
Peerless Entertainers, The, 15, 17

Ralna and Guy, 94, 96
Ralston, Bob, 83, 103
Ramsey, Curt, 80
Ramsay, Helen, 54
Renner, Fern (Mrs. Lawrence Welk) 19–20
    childhood, ·21
    marriage, 20
Roberts, Jimmy, 77, 83, 103–104

Sandi and Salli, 73, 78
Schalk, Frank, 14
Semonski Sisters, the, 79
Smale, Bob, 83
Smart, Doug, 80
Sullivan, Kathie, 80, 91–92
Szell, Johnny, 80

Walton, Jayne, 53
Weiss, Rose, 69
Welk, Agatha, 10
Welk, Ann Mary, 10
Welk, Barbara, 10
Welk, Christina, 9
Welk, Donna Lee, 23
Welk, Eva, 10
Welk, John, 10
Welk, Kevin, 70
Welk, Lawrence,
    birth, 10
    business empire, 49
    childhood, 9
    daily routine, 50
    education, 12
    marriage, 20
    radio shows, 17, 22
    recordings, 109–110
    television career, 31, 34–36, 39–40
Welk, Lawrence, Jr. 24, 64, 68, 70
Welk, Lawrence, III, 70
Welk, Louie, 10
Welk, Ludwig, 9

Youth Opportunity Plan, 46, 78

Zall, Hohn, 83
Zimmer, Norma, 62, 82, 84–85
    children, 84
    grandchildren, 84
Zimmer Randy, 62, 84

(Memory Shop)